"I love this book! Wisdom and wit worth remembering and sharing."

Josh Berman, *Creator and Executive Producer,* Drop Dead Diva *and* Notorious

"It would be a 'Shame' if the humor and inspiration from these wise women was lost. Dr. Lois captured their spirits in a book to share with every woman in your family. This is truly a good read."

Award-Winning R&B and Disco Singer, Evelyn Champagne King

"It's about time for a book like this. For too long the wisdom of older women has gone unnoticed, unappreciated, and undervalued. *Ageless Women, Timeless Wisdom* is sure to put a smile on your face and the faces of the women you share it with."

Singer/Songwriter, Rita Coolidge

A portion of the proceeds from all book sales goes to Bloom Again Foundation, a nonprofit organization providing working women living at the poverty level with rapid response financial assistance when they encounter medical challenges that cause them to miss work.

Also by Dr. Lois Frankel

Women, Anger & Depression

Kindling the Spirit

Overcoming Your Strengths

Nice Girls Don't Get the Corner Office

Nice Girls Don't Get Rich

Stop Sabotaging Your Career

Nice Girls Just Don't Get It (with Carol Frohlinger)

Also by Lisa Graves

A Thyme and Place: Medieval Feasts and Recipes for the Modern Table

History's Witches, an Illustrated Guide

Trail Blazers, an Illustrated Guide to the Women Who Explored the World

Her Majesty, an Illustrated Guide to the Women Who Ruled the World

Colorful Women in History, a Coloring Book

The Witches, a Coloring Book

AGELESS WOMEN, TIMELESS WISDOM

*Witty, Wicked, and Wise
Reflections on Well-Lived Lives*

Written by Dr. Lois Frankel
Illustrated by Lisa Graves

Skyhorse Publishing

Skyhorse Publishing books may be purchased in bulk at special discounts for sales promotion, corporate gifts, fund-raising, or educational purposes. Special editions can also be created to specifications. For details, contact the Special Sales Department, Skyhorse Publishing, 307 West 36th Street, 11th Floor, New York, NY 10018 or info@skyhorsepublishing.com.

Skyhorse® and Skyhorse Publishing® are registered trademarks of Skyhorse Publishing, Inc.®, a Delaware corporation.

Visit our website at www.skyhorsepublishing.com.

10 9 8 7 6 5 4

Library of Congress Cataloging-in-Publication Data is available on file.

Cover design by Lisa Graves
Cover photo credit by Lois P. Frankel, PhD

Print ISBN: 978-1-5107-1624-7
Ebook ISBN: 978-1-5107-1626-1

Printed in China

This book is dedicated to my mother, Sonia Kriss Frankel.
I wish I had the opportunity to tell her that I finally know
just how wise she really was.

AGELESS WOMEN, TIMELESS ADVICE

Witty, Wicked, and Wise Reflections on Well-Lived Lives

For the unlearned, old age is winter. For the learned, it is the season of the harvest. —Hasidic Proverb

There is a sign that has hung in my office for many years: *Entrance to another's soul is a sacred honor.* It is a reminder that as a psychotherapist, executive coach, and, now, documenter of women's unique lives, I have a responsibility to treat what is shared (whether across the couch, across the desk, or across the ocean) as precious. Listening to the stories of the women interviewed for this book as they spoke about where they came from and how they got to be where they are now, I was touched by the trust they placed in me with their most treasured possessions—their memories. Quite honestly, I had no idea how richly and deeply their experiences would transform my world. Not only did I learn to be more patient (not something for which I am known), but also more curious, compassionate, and courageous. I was inspired to take action on several other projects I had been thinking about but not quite sure about embracing. I'm hoping that reading this book may have the same impact on you as well!

For the purpose of this book I chose to focus on septuagenarian, octogenarian, nonagenarian, and even a few centenarian women. In other words, women from seventy to a hundred years old. Every effort was made to include a wide spectrum of women with different backgrounds, ethnicities, educational experiences, and religions. Some had married and lived decades raising children and sometimes grandchildren, caring for ill husbands and parents, creating "nests" from which progeny fly out of to be productive members of society, and often being forced to observe more than participate in the events around them. Other women that I spoke with chose not to marry or have children and instead had careers outside of the home, traveled extensively, or ran their own businesses. Yet others chose religious paths and spent their lives educating generations of children, caring for the poor, or ministering to the sick. Regardless of their past, every woman had valuable insights, perspectives, and experiences from which we can all learn.

As a society, however, we often fail to capitalize on that wisdom. Instead, we marginalize women who no longer look like Madison Avenue's definition of vibrant and relevant and overlook the myriad ways in which their existence is actually essential to the survival of us all. As a result, older women theselves often don't recognize and acknowledge the ways in which their contributions are still valuable. So, the process of gleaning their wisdom took longer than I anticipated. It wasn't as simple as asking a question and receiving an answer, it was about first listening to their stories. Woven between the lines of long lives were pearls of wisdom hard-earned from life experiences as unique as seemingly identical snowflakes, only to find under closer examination just how inimitable each one is.

Unfortunately most people tend to lump all older women into the same homogeneous pile when nothing could be further from the truth. They are as different in maturity as they were in their youth. Curious young women continue to take classes on subjects like the Byzantine Empire and the History of the American Railroad well into their nineties. Social-minded young women become mature women who volunteer for hospice or to teach immigrant women how to read. And adventurous young women continue to seek challenges to conquer with grit and determination. The stories I collected from women around the world reflect these differences in temperament, background, experiences, and interests.

Listening to them was not only inspirational, it was also a lesson in history. From ninety-one year old Peggy Kennell I learned about the Johnstown Flood of 1936. Eighty-six-year-old Wai-Ling Lew taught me about the Chinese Exclusion Act of 1882 that barred the immigration of all Chinese laborers. And Yvonne Richmond, eighty-one years old, illuminated what it was like for an African American to live through the race riots of the 1960s.

In retrospect, I see now that my original vision for this book as a sweet little homage to the homespun wisdom of older women was totally misguided by my own blind spots about older women. The vision began to change when I started actually interviewing and speaking with as many women as I could. Then there were the submissions from the daughters, sons, granddaughters, and nieces and nephews of women who had heard about the project and wanted to submit something from the older women in their lives, both living and having passed away. The first one to give me pause was the one from a young man who said whenever he would procrastinate his mother would tell him, "Yeah, and if your aunt had balls she'd be your uncle." What am I supposed to do with that? I wondered, but filed it away.

A short time later I met Jo-Ann Mercurio in a pet boutique in Palm Springs, California, asked her what she knew to be true after all of her years of living and she replied, "If life gives you lemons . . . look for the vodka." Hmmm. Not quite what I was expecting. Then, asking Nina Vincente in Scottsdale, Arizona the same question, I got the reply, "Don't trust men. If they don't treat you well, leave them. They don't change." Good advice as well, but different from what I thought she might say. So, I decided to go with the flow and incorporate everything I learned, whether I agreed with it or not, whether it was religious or irreverent, and whether it was sweet or sour. Everything wound up being grist for this mill.

There was one other variation from my original plan that you might find interesting. The original title for this book was *Words of Wisdom from Wise Old Women*. I was on a personal crusade to destigmatize the phrase *old woman*. Younger women loved the title but older women? No so much. They don't see themselves as the stereotype of old age and they want others to acknowledge their ongoing relevance and vitality. As ninety-one-year-old Dorie Snedeker told me as we were saying good-bye, "I'm 39 from the neck up but 139 from neck down."

So, ladies, I heard you and agree—you are indeed ageless and endowed with timeless wisdom. Thanks for sharing!

People cannot expect
to ask for more than a
thousand good days just
as a flower cannot be
expected to maintain its
red color for more than
a hundred days.

Wanda Wang | June 16, 1937
Shanghai, China

Better to throw unhealthy
food in the trash than put it in your
body! Follow Zsa Zsa and
find a rich man. Put cream on
your elbows. Refined women
with class have nice and
smooth elbows.

Frances Yousanoff Mazerov | 1915
Persia
Died: 1996

Do not be scared
of the world.
Make the world
scared of you.

Luisa Vincente

November 6, 1892
Laucera, Italy
Died: January 16, 1975

Patience is a virtue.
Try to remember that
you have the internal
and external resources
to handle anything
that comes your way.

Connie Bertolone Picascia

August 20, 1922
Trenton, New Jersey
Died: April 16, 2013

Change is the one constant. Don't waste your time looking for stability. Stay open to whatever happens.

Eleanor Moffat | October 10, 1931
Sharon, Pennsylvania

See the world.

Stella Loughran | September 14, 1930
Tipperary, Ireland

Love is never wrong; it has only one purpose: happiness. But never put your love in the hands of the wrong person. Especially in the hands of the person who already has a soulmate. Disaster will surely follow.

Sri Kartini Abrahim | September 23, 1934
Subang, Indonesia

Born in Ching Lung Lei, a tiny village in southern China, Mrs. Lew (as she prefers to be called) was an only child. Although China's one-child policy was initiated in the 1950s, it was not the reason her mother had no other children. She was an only child because her father had left China to seek his fortune in Mexico as an overseas sojourner laborer before she was born. Mrs. Lew wouldn't meet him until she was twenty years old. Each month, with the exception of one period during World War II, her father would write and send money to support his small family. While in Mexico he started another family. This was not uncommon and known to all parties involved during this period.

Life was difficult in the tiny village. There was no electricity and the nearest communal toilet was a ways down the dusty road. In those days women did not work in business but rather took care of children and the household. There was famine, and many young men sought fortunes beyond China to work overseas. Those who remained, the "bad guys," as she called them, knew which families were single-mother households and targeted them for burglaries.

As World War II spread to Asia, money became scarce with the interruption of mail service. Danger from the Japanese occupation lurked. Her mother decided it was safer to move to Macau, a Portuguese colony across the Pearl River Delta from Hong Kong. There her mother worked first as a seamstress to augment what little money was sent by her husband and soon she opened her own shop. Mrs. Lew also worked in the shop, and by the age of fourteen she could sew an entire custom-made dress in one day. It was there that Mrs. Lew learned how to manage money and a household. You see, despite being poor and uneducated, her

mother was smart and shrewd. She saved every little bit of money she possibly could (from her husband's allowance and her own savings as a seamstress), and when she had acquired enough, she wisely invested and managed real estate in Hong Kong.

When World War II ended and Mrs. Lew had graduated from the equivalent of high school, her mother offered her a choice: go to work or continue with higher education. Mrs. Lew chose education and studied accounting in Canton University. When asked why she chose accounting, she replied, "I had to learn something to do something." Having watched her mother manage her own businesses and investments, accounting was a logical choice.

Somewhere early in her collegiate years, her father returned to Hong Kong from Mexico, and this was when they met for the first time. She was afraid of the quiet man who didn't speak much. She didn't really know him. And, as is customary in the Chinese culture, people do not openly display physical or emotional affection. It was only much later, toward the end of her father's life, that she felt closer to him. Much of this was the result of him conversing with her as an adult to another adult, contributing to her understanding of him and helping her come to terms with their relationship.

When Mrs. Lew completed college, her mother decided it was time to live with her husband in Mexico. Faced again with another defining life choice, Mrs. Lew followed her mother. Her father put her to work in his restaurant, where she met her half-siblings for the first time. Yet the entire time she and her mother lived in Mexico, they never met her father's other wife. He deliberately kept the two wives and households separate.

Mrs. Lew's college boyfriend soon traveled to join them in Mexico. As it turned out, he had also never met his father, a merchant in Monterey, California. Since Mexico was a lot closer to California than Hong Kong, he would be able to locate his father easily from there. Eventually he found his father, but because he was over twenty-one, his father could not sponsor him to immigrate to the U.S.

Soon, Mrs. Lew and her boyfriend married and started their own family in Mexico. The couple would have three daughters. Her husband insisted that the children be born in the U.S., so when the eighth month of pregnancy approached they boarded a rickety plane and flew to Los Angeles to stay with his father and siblings. Mrs. Lew's daughters were born on U.S. soil, making them citizens of the United States. Then back they returned to Mexico where she stayed home raising their children while her husband worked in her father's restaurant.

When the girls reached school age, Mrs. Lew said her daughters should be educated and gave her husband a choice of residency—Hong Kong, Mexico, or the U.S. By then, President Kennedy had made it easier for immigrants to come to the U.S. if they had a sibling sponsor residing there. Her husband's eldest brother stepped up to become their sponsor.

Once in Los Angeles, the young family lived sparsely. Her husband worked at a Chinese grocery store where, she said, he wasn't very happy. He was used to having more autonomy in her father's restaurant. With her encouragement, they opened their own Chinese restaurant in North Hollywood, California. Following her mother's example, Mrs. Lew saved her pennies until the couple could invest in their own real estate. They bought apartment houses where they could live and manage the property.

The most touching part of Mrs. Lew's story was a promise she made to her father. On his deathbed, he asked that she, as the eldest of all his children, promise to take care of his second family. This was a family she had not grown up with, and she had only developed some connection with them during the few years she lived in Mexico. At this point, she hadn't even met her father's other wife. Nonetheless, true to her word and honoring her father's wishes, Mrs. Lew sent funds to this other wife for over twenty years. When asked why she would be so generous to someone she didn't even know, she replied softly, "Because I didn't want her to have to live the kind of life I lived during the war when we got no money from my father."

And what advice does she have to give others?
Only reluctantly does she give any advice, but it's this:

Education is very important. If you're not educated, even if you work hard, you will have a difficult time achieving your goals. If you are educated, but you don't work hard, you won't achieve your goals. But if you are educated and work hard, you will be successful.

 August 18, 1940
Los Angeles, California

I hear women say they could never tell their partner this or that. Neither you nor your spouse or partner is made out of chocolate. It is possible to share confessions or disappointments without melting. Experiencing conflict by speaking truthfully and working to resolve it can bring you closer together.

Heather Thomas | August 19, 1934
Melbourne, Australia

Do things while you can, when you can—because that time might not come around again. An example? My husband and I weren't sure if we wanted to go overseas again, and we were waiting—and then he had an accident and now he can't travel. So take all the opportunities when you can!

My mother always used to ask, "Are you having any fun?" Now that I'm eighty-six, I appreciate that question even more.

Minerva Canavan | 1928
St. Louis, Missouri

Be strong. If you have to be alone, be alone.
You always have yourself. Your spirit. Be optimistic.
No man ever gave me even one single dollar.

Nina Vincente | December 3, 1934
Puglia, Italy

*While traveling the Southern tier of the United States
to collect wisdom from women with whom I would
never otherwise cross paths, my friend Linda Carpenter
called to tell me she met the most fascinating woman
and asked if I wanted to interview her. Trusting Linda's
judgment, we scheduled a time when we could both
talk to Nina Vincente while I was passing through
Phoenix, Arizona. Linda was right. Nina is nothing less
than a force of nature. Speaking with a heavy Italian accent, at times it was impossible to tell if she was
speaking in English or Italian. In fact, it was a little of
both but she had no problem getting her point across
and we had no problem understanding her. Her story
was peppered with frequently asking "capito?" Nina
held court for three hours—and they were three of the
most spellbound hours of my life.*

*To say that Nina is effervescent is an understatement.
No taller than five feet and maybe 110 pounds soaking
wet, she said her mother used to tell her "the smaller
the barrel, the better the wine"—the Italian version
of the maxim "good things come in small packages."
I would describe her as Gina Lollobrigida meets Estelle
Getty from* The Golden Girls. *Her home is filled with
pictures of her younger self—all of them voluptuous and
many of them seductive. As her story reveals, Nina is
a woman who knew how to get what she wanted and,
most of the time, wanted what she got.*

I was a queen in Italy. I had three restaurants, two bou-
tiques, and a discotheque. To do this you have to treat
people nice. I've had people work for me for thirty-five
years. Men are superficial. I'm deep. I learned to be
independent when the town we lived in was gone from
bombing during World War II. It was in ruins. My mother
said we had to be tough. So we went to the mountains
until it was all over. When we went back to Puglia, it was
all gone. That taught me I have to take care of myself.

I went to San Remo when I was about twenty-six or
twenty-seven years old to open a restaurant with money
given to me by my Mamma and grandmother. I learned
how to cook from watching my Mamma in her restaurant
from the time I was a little girl. I also knew how to sew.
At seventeen, I learned how to make pants. My brain told
me I could make money sewing pants—everyone needs
pants—but my love was cooking.

You don't have to go to school to cook in Italy. You
make good food at home. Three generations were cooks.
I said I have to cook too. When I make chicken, people
go crazy—it's only chicken! The Sicilians put too much
in their foods. It's why they get ulcers. Mine is simple.
I slept only three hours a night preparing everything
I had to get ready for the next day. Nina Italiana was
the name of my first restaurant.

I was in San Remo for five years when I knew I wanted
children but I didn't want to get married. I also had my
ovaries removed six months earlier. I wanted a baby so
badly. There was a Swedish man who was a tour guide
and he would always bring tourists to the restaurant
when he was in town. He was beautiful. His name was
Tom. I introduced myself to him. We became friends.
One night he invited me to a dance. We fell in love and
it exploded that night. We started to date. One night I
invited him to my apartment. In the lift going up I was

19

talking to myself about going to bed with him. I figured I couldn't get pregnant, so we made love.

A month later I went to the doctor and said I felt strange. I wanted to eat all the time and I was vomiting. The smell of food made me sick and I had to cook all day! The doctor told me to come back in two weeks and when I did, he did a urine test. I thought he was going to tell me I had a tumor and I was upset. Instead, I was pregnant! I was a miracle woman! They had missed a little bit of the ovary, and because I'm an active woman it grew back.

When I told Tom, he wanted to get married. But I didn't. I had many admirers who wanted to marry me but I didn't want to be oppressed. I could see how in other marriages both spouses were oppressed. My father died during the war so I grew up with no daddy. Tom took me to meet his family. They were Jewish. His mother was an angel. She asked me if I would be willing to raise the baby Jewish. I told her I couldn't because I was Catholic, but I wasn't a fanatic Catholic. I asked her what else I could do to make her happy with this baby, and she said she wanted the baby circumcised. Bingo! I said fine. It's cleaner that way anyway. When my water broke I put a tablecloth in the car (I had a Jaguar and didn't want to ruin it) and drove myself to the hospital. Tom and I remain friends, and he acted as a father to our son. He was involved in our son's life.

The years pass. Five years later I had a big wedding party at my restaurant and they brought in a band. This one boy with the band was beautiful. He was half my age. I wanted a child with him. I told Jesus I wanted a little girl with this boy. But I didn't see him again. Then one day, I needed to have some drapes put into my apartment and I had a workman come. He was this short little guy. Really unattractive. After we discussed it he told me he would send his son Leonardo to take measurements for the drapes the next day. When the son showed up it was the beautiful boy! I said, "Jesus kissed you!" I was crazy.

Going up to my apartment in the lift, the boy is shaking. He's scared. He takes the measurements and leaves. When he comes back to put up the drapes, I tell him not to be scared. To tell me what he really wants. It's okay to tell me. He said he wants to make love to me. It was his first time. We make love and one month later, I'm pregnant again. He wanted to get married but I only wanted to be his fantasy-come-true. He kept calling me Signora. I told him to stop with that and call me Nina! I told Leonardo that he didn't have to tell his parents that I was pregnant, but he wanted to. And they wanted us to get married too. I was well-known and wealthy. I loved him and I wanted to be with him, but I didn't want to get married. I've always been eccentric. We spent several years together and he was a good father to our daughter. But my destiny was to come to America.

In 1974 a friend invited me to go to a disco one night, and when I walked in I saw this beautiful [biracial] man with large eyes. He walked over to me and asked if I spoke English. I looked at him and wondered if this was finally the man I could marry. At the end of the evening I invited him to come to the boutique to look at the jeans I had. When he came in and I saw him, I said, "This man is mine!" We dated for two weeks, then James and I went to the American Consulate and got married. I felt love so deep for him I didn't want anyone else there. It was just me and him. I love the men who gave me the gift of my children, but this man was different.

A few weeks later, we moved to the U.S. He was in the military and had to have his last assignment at his home base in Phoenix before he could retire. I wanted to open a restaurant but he didn't want me to, so I didn't. Soon he started coming home from work at different times or coming home late. I knew he wasn't coming right from work. I asked him if there was another woman, and he said there wasn't. But the next morning after he left for work, I packed his bags and put them outside. My children wanted to know what happened to him but I couldn't let him stay in my life. He broke my heart. He taught me never to trust men again. People tried talking me into taking him back but I couldn't. I was in pain. I had sworn never to marry, but I did.

I didn't speak with him for many years. Then one day, a beautiful little [biracial] girl knocked on my door. I asked her who had sent her and she looked toward a parked car. There was James and his new wife. When he got out of the car I could see he was disabled. He had difficulty walking. I invited them all into my home, and we have remained friends since then.

What have you learned over the course of your life?

Be strong. If you have to be alone, be alone. You always have yourself. Your spirit. Be optimistic. No man ever gave me even one single dollar.

What advice would you give a young woman today?

Be like me. Don't trust men too much. If they don't treat you well, leave them. They don't change.

Be good to yourself,
take care of your health,
and see as much of the
world as you can.

Marilyn Connor | July 22, 1927
Quincy, Massachusetts

Ellie Newbauer

June 16, 1925
Harbor Creek, Pennsylvania

Until she reached nearly fifty years old, Eleanor Newbauer was the daughter, wife, and mother she was taught to be growing up on a farm during the depression. Although she never made it past tenth grade, she was always smart, creative, courageous, and driven. After listening to her story I was inspired to go out and do some things I had been putting off because I thought it was too late in life to do them. She continues to be a mentor and guide to women of all ages and still has things yet to do before she can rest.

The messages I got from my mother were things like don't get a swelled head and don't act very important—the old harangue that all of us from that generation got about making yourself as small as you could be. You were supposed to give to everyone else and what was left you could have. The role of women was to stay home and take care of the house. The boys were supposed to go out and get a job as soon as they graduated from high school and prepare themselves to support a family.

I went as far as the tenth grade and then worked at the five and dime store. By seventeen years old I was married to a young man I met in high school. He was nineteen. Some of this was due to coming from a big family and growing up during the depression. We had no money. I was four years old when the depression started. We lived on a farm so we had food. We learned to do with what we had and make it last. People throw out more food today that we could use to feed the world.

My marriage was traditional. I had my first child at eighteen. We were married in October and John left in January, 1943 for World War II. He was gone for two and a half years. I had the baby during that time and was living with Mom and Dad. Then they decided to move to Florida and I thought, *no way*. John asked me to put $600 in the bank for him, but instead I used it to buy a house that I found. That house cost $6,500. My sister paid room and board and with the $50 a month I got from the government it paid for the mortgage. I made it for two years, keeping everything afloat while John was in the service. When he came back we sold that house in 1949 for $10,500 and bought another house in the country for $10,000.

Once John came home from service, he became the man of the house, which was the way it was then, and I became the "little wife." On the one hand it was frustrating, and on the other hand I didn't have to worry about anything else. He worked and I stayed home and took care of the house. I just kept myself busy and didn't get resentful. I'd think, *look what you've got, stop complaining*. And this went on until I was fifty-one. We had four kids altogether and it took a lot of time to raise them. I was busy with women's club and all the stuff that women who don't work do. Later on I would play bridge. I was busy.

When I was in my late forties, I was having lunch with friends and I said, "I am so bored with my life I'm going to change everything." I started by changing my name from Eleanor to Ellie. Eleanor is reserved and queenly whereas Ellie is outgoing and social. It's amazing how people relate to their names. Changing names will change your personality! When you relate differently to your name, everyone else does too.

At fifty-one, I opened a shop, Ellie's Gifts and Old Things, and ran it for eight years. I bought it on April

Fools' Day and sold it on April Fools' Day. John immediately took over the bookkeeping and finances, which I resented because I wanted it to be a project of my own. But he must have figured I didn't know enough about money. I did everything else. I bought and sold everything in the store. When John retired he wanted to travel, and you can't travel and own a business, so I sold it. We used the money to buy a house at the lake and a motor home on the same day.

In 1990, John had a bypass and he was sick after that. He was on so much medication he was a zombie. He passed away in 2000. He could take care of himself but he wasn't interested in anything but watching television. It was during this period I started hearing voices and started channeling. One night, in the middle of the night, I was awake but I wasn't aware. I was semiconscious between wake and sleep. And I heard as clearly as I'm talking to you a voice: "I will give you the laws of the universe."

I thought I could have been losing my mind. It was kind of weird. When I told my husband that I had a wonderful dream, he dismissed it. A couple nights later it happened again, and the voices started talking about the laws of nature. It became a nightly thing. I wasn't frightened. It was like sitting at the feet of a master and I was in awe. I couldn't believe it was happening to me. I told the voices that I couldn't remember what was said at night and asked, "Can you come during the day during mediation so I can write down what you're telling me?" Which is what they did.

I have no clue if it's part of myself, but they call themselves the Teachers and they simply teach. Depending on the questions being asked, you can hear and feel their different energy as each one answers.

A teacher who is proficient at whatever is being asked is the one to respond. My husband thought I was nuts, so I called a friend and asked if she'd come and tell me what she thought. She said she thought we needed to get a discussion group together. We had nine people and we met twice a month. We called ourselves The Seekers. The group would ask questions and I would allow the answers to come through me. After I did this, I was energized. This went on for about twelve to fifteen years at our house on Cedar Crest in Richmond, Virginia. After John died, the group started coming down to the lake. The Seekers were spiritual, inspirational. Most of them have died now.

When John died, it took me four months to even realize he was gone. I expected to see him coming around the corner. Then one day, I realized he was not going to be there. I was walking one day and I met this neighbor who said that when her husband died, she thought, *I could be a widow or I could be an artist. And I chose to be an artist.* I thought, *that is exactly right, and I decided I would be a mentor and a writer.* And that's what I do. I added an addition to the lake house in 2004 and I did workshops and retreats for five years until I got tired and stopped doing that. They were self-awareness workshops. One of them was called, "Who Am I? The Art of Selfishness."

I write books about what I know and about life itself. I don't write channeled books. There are too many out there and we don't need another one. I mentor people who come to see me. I'm a sounding board and I say back to them what they're saying. And I let them figure out what they need. Everyone knows what they need to do but they don't hear themselves or trust themselves. So when they hear it said back to them, they think it's so wise! *How did you come up with that*, they wonder. It's just what they said themselves.

I started a first Sunday group where everyone is welcome and it's an open discussion. Sometimes there is a speaker and sometimes not. Both men and women come. I just throw out something to talk about. Never anything political or religious. That has grown from six to thirty people. On every third Saturday I started the Women's Open Forum for just women, to help them find their potential. It's to inspire women to get on with what they want to do rather than with what they think they have to do. I have fifty on my mailing list. Women speakers come in who may have had a challenge. They talk about their lives and what they did to get their dreams on track. Women think they have to be there for everyone else, but I think we are important enough to be here along with everyone else. There is a board of young, gung-ho women for the forum. After this year, I will step down from the board and let them take it over.

I'm looking to sell the lake house now, but I still want to buy a place where women can meet. I'd like to build cottages for people to write or be creative and rent out the cottages. I found a place, but it's half a million dollars. That's a vision I have for that particular group. I intend for it to continue way beyond my time. For me, I'm going to get a small, little, tiny house and write and play.

On Aging

My body is ninety, but I'm going on forty in my thinking. If my body would agree with me, there are a lot of things I would like to do. I give everyone else my ideas and let them do it. By ninety, your body doesn't want to get up and go any more. It just wants to sit and read. The mind controls your entire life. What you think is what you create. If you think only with your mind, then you're not creating out of your heart. The heart has so much intelligence. Let the heart be the CEO and the brain be the president who puts into action what the heart is telling it to do. The mind is the vice president. The mind takes in everything in the outer world; it tells you what you should do. The heart tells you what your destiny is and what you need to do to fill your soul. It's where your soul is. Your brain simply does the work of bringing it into fruition. The mind is the worker; it goes about seeing how it can happen. It brings in everything from the outer world to make it happen. The mind collects everything you need to know to fill the heart's desire, who you need to meet, and what you need to do.

Aging is wonderful. I wouldn't go back a day. It's exciting to think about it. It's what you are doing right now in this moment that's important because it's all you have and it's creating your future. The past will sometimes rule because the path sets the patterns for our life, but if we start thinking about something we want to create differently in this moment, it's what creates your future. Aging seems to be the ultimate failure in the thinking of youth. It appears that without that seeming failure, we would all be dead.

Youth is transient. Youth, as soon as you think she's yours, will turn her back on you. She's fickle that way. Stop looking in the mirror. The mirror will lie to you every time. Don't be dependent on your body telling you who you are. It has no clue.

If you were born to be shot you won't be drowned.

Hannah Moran | November 13, 1921
Aglish, Ireland
Died: November 27, 2011

Live, love, laugh, and be
happy but do it in the Lord's way.
Don't preach to your husband.
They don't listen anyway.

Betty Nelson | February 29, 1932
Kodiak Island, Alaska

You are what you make it.

Edna Keefer | May 27, 1929
La Puente, California
Died: November 25, 2006

Live life to the fullest; enjoy life.
Only marry for love.

Anne Babasick | September 9, 1924
Greenville, South Carolina

Nancy Gray

November 11, 1932
South Portland, Maine

Are you Ms. Gray?
I was when I woke up this morning!

And so began my fireside chat with the grand dame of the New England hospitality industry, eighty-three-year-old Nancy Dyer Gray. Small and unassuming, it would be easy to mistake her for one of the guests at her Harraseeket Inn in Freeport, Maine. But looks can deceive. Make no mistake about it, this is one shrewd businesswoman who has bought, sold, and built inns of all sizes for nearly five decades. In the inevitable skirmishes that have ensued over the years, it sometimes looked like Bambi vs. Godzilla—and Bambi usually prevailed. "She's tougher than a bag of hammers," remarked son Chip Gray who sat with us to help prompt her now fading memories.

Nancy started her career in hospitality in 1945 at the ripe old age of twelve. She worked at her parent's sporting camps on Holeb Pond (a remote area of Western Maine not far from the Canadian border) as a waitress, dishwasher, cook's helper, and window cleaner. That first summer season, Nancy made $500 in tips, in addition to her $8 a week paycheck—no small amount in those days. "Working is very educational. Even hard work can be fun. When you connect with people you learn from them," she advised. Perhaps that's what makes Nancy so wise—she connects with people on a deep and genuine level in that down-to-earth, New Englander sort of way.

Although she studied to become a dental hygienist, after marrying her husband, Paul, she worked full time helping her parents run an inn they had purchased in Gloucester, Massachusetts. By then she had four children, and when her father unexpectedly died after buying another inn in Mystic, Connecticut, she found herself back in the innkeeping business full time. Along with her sister, Jody, Nancy was instrumental in taking the inn at Mystic from bankruptcy to a world-renowned boutique hotel. "The bankers didn't want to give me any money because I was a woman," she remembers. "My husband had to put our home up as collateral." The sisters took a run-down forty-room motel and turned it into seventeen-acres of beauty overlooking the ocean.

Is it a challenge being a woman in an industry dominated by men? "It's a greater challenge raising kids," she said. "The problem is that doesn't come with any lessons. So you just raise your kids the way you were raised and hope for the best." After thinking about it for a moment more, she added, "The only challenge I've had in my business is mechanical or physical. When you have to lift something heavy, you call the boys in." And some of the boys in the business didn't want Nancy as a part of their club. But that didn't stop her from ultimately being not only invited to sit on the prestigious Resort Committee of the American Hotel and Lodging Association but also serving as its first woman chairperson. "She sat elbow to elbow with the likes of Michael Eisner, Donald Trump, and other big hoteliers," her son Chip proudly points out. "She's too modest to say it, but she really is a visionary. She can see things no one else can see." Part of that vision came in the form of being an early advocate for environmentally sound practices in the hotel industry.

Having grown up in the woods, she has a healthy respect for the land and its inhabitants, both human and otherwise. As the story goes, her father taught her to be an excellent marksman with a shotgun. One day, as a young girl showing off with some friends, she shot a squirrel. Looking at its lifeless body, she vowed to never again shoot an animal—and she never did.

Nancy has spent a lifetime supporting land preservation, water quality, and animal protection issues, serving on several local and statewide commissions and working in the trenches. This hasn't always made her friends.

A lot of people want you to mind your own business and keep your mouth shut. It's important to have a desire to make things better or at least not let them get any worse. To do this you have to be truthful.

The two keys to a long and successful marriage are that you both must have a good sense of humor and you must live a really long time.

Julia Louise Moore Morris | October 13, 1920
Wooster, Ohio
Died: November 16, 2008

Life is too short for
quibbling and arguing,
particularly with
people you love.

Virginia MacCracken Hunter | 1918
Beatrice, Nebraska
Died: May 31, 2014

Awake to the magic of
life. Each day is a miracle.
We only have to be open,
see it, and live it.

Charlotte Sherman | June 18, 1924
Los Angeles, California

Sister Jean Schmidt

August 21, 1919
San Francisco, California

If you get a great job but you don't like it, quit.
You don't want to be a pain to yourself and everyone else.

My Great Uncle Godfrey returned from World War I terribly disfigured from stepping on a landmine. While recovering in a military hospital, he met a wise woman named Helen Harriet Skinner. They fell in love and got married. As a preteen I asked her how she could fall in love with a man so disfigured. She replied simply: "You have to love the man more than the package he comes in."

Helen Harriet Skinner MacKenzie

March 21, 1928
Madison, Wisconsin
Died: April 8, 1991

Don't take any shit and always have a stash of get-away money that your husband doesn't know about.

Catherine Marie Ebner | September 12, 1899
Medina, New York
Died: December 27, 1988

Her last words before she passed away: "Let's get this over with."

Clarabelle Goodrich | June 6, 1919
San Antonio, Texas
Died: November, 2014

WHEN LIFE GIVES YOU LEMONS . . . ADD VODKA.

Jo-Ann Mercurio | September 9, 1941
Los Angeles, California

It's important to have a moral compass to live a moral life.

Elaine Booth | October 1, 1931
Nice, France

Compassion gives freedom to your heart. Always have compassion for everything and everybody, no matter how simple or small it is. Compassion helps you to understand the reason for everything so you can help people with kindness and humanism.

María Teresa Cruz Reyes | 1920
Toluca, Estado de México

Be true to your feelings. Honor how you feel. If you feel sad and someone tells you not to be, don't listen to them.

Jean Wilkinson | July 10, 1925
Hollywood, California

I should have known this would be no ordinary interview when I scheduled it with Jean's daughter, Lynn. She suggested that we meet at the Smokehouse Restaurant in Toluca Lake, California. Which was fine, but when she added, "This is where we go to celebrate; we celebrated losing my virginity here," I was more than a little surprised. "You celebrated losing your virginity with your MOTHER?" I asked. "Oh yeah. And the next day Mom took me to get birth control pills," she added. When I walked into the restaurant Jean was already seated at the table and I couldn't quite reconcile this sweet, old, twinkly-eyed woman to the stories of a woman who was so open-minded about her daughter's first sexual experience before she was even out of high school. But you can never judge a book by its cover, and that turned out to be the least of my surprises with Jean Wilkinson.

Born in Hollywood, California, to a father who played viola with the Los Angeles Philharmonic, Jean was an only child. "Working as a musician Dad was only employed six months of the year, so Mother really learned how to stretch a dollar. She made all of my clothes. I didn't have a store-bought dress until I went to college," she explained. This arrangement, with Jean's mother staying home to care for her daughter and making do all year long with only a half year's income, enabled her father to pursue his passion for music. "Dad really didn't have much concern about money," she said. And so, like in so many families, the woman enables the husband to do what he wants while she keeps the home fires burning.

"It's hard to image now, but growing up in Hollywood during World War II was a safe place. We didn't lock our doors. It was family oriented," Jean remembered. "I went to Hollywood High School. The only person who went on to fame in my school that I can remember was Richard Jaeckel, who became an actor." After graduation she went to the University of Southern California on a full music performance scholarship. "This meant in exchange for tuition I would perform at campus events and for visiting dignitaries as a coloratura soprano," she explained. And it was there she met her future husband, Bob, who in many ways defined the woman she ultimately became.

"After college I was hired as the first music director at the classical radio station KUSC. Along with Bob, we founded the Burbank Unitarian Fellowship. Later I served as District Executive of the Pacific Southwest District of the Unitarian Universalist Association doing fundraising, leadership training, and conflict resolution," Jean said of her professional history. But it is clearly her unconventional relationship with Bob that dominates her memories. They were married for fifty years before he passed away in 2000. Asked the secret to such a long marriage she replied, "Tenacity." And then the real story started . . .

"We were married in 1950. And those first years, it was a great marriage. We had a daughter and a son and would take the kids on trips to San Diego and Santa Barbara. We'd go kite flying," Jean remembers fondly. "Then one day, Bob read the book *Sex Without Guilt* by Albert Ellis, the gist of which was you could love more than one person at a time. It was the 1960s and the beginning of the sexual revolution."

Bob suggested that they try out an "open marriage"— one where they could each have intimate relationships outside of their marriage. Jean wanted no part of it. But Bob persisted, and like any good wife of her generation, she not only wanted to make her husband happy, she thought she had no choice in the matter. In her mind, leaving him wasn't an option. By now, they had two small children and she had few skills

that would allow her to find a job that would pay her enough to raise them as she wanted. Like her mother before her, Jean was a dutiful wife. "I did what I had to do," she shrugged. "I was afraid of being alone."

For the next twelve years, Jean had what she described as meaningful serially monogamous relationships. "I thought since everyone else was doing it, I should too," she said. "Then it stopped working for me. My sex life with my husband was practically nonexistent. We slept in separate bedrooms." When the experiment in open marriage began, they had an agreement that if either one of them wanted to end the arrangement, it would be over. When Jean told Bob she wanted it to end, he agreed.

But Bob didn't keep up his end of the agreement. For two more years, he maintained the open marriage relationship he had already been in. Following the end of this relationship there was a dry spell, and sometime later he started an eighteen-year relationship that Jean only learned about after Bob died. Although she had her suspicions, perhaps she didn't really want

to know. There were certainly clues. For example, Bob wasn't a smoker, and when she asked him why the car smelled like cigarette smoke, he would say it was from some people from work he had given a lift to, when in fact it was his lover who smoked.

After he retired, Bob was often gone on what he described as business-related trips. After his death, when cleaning out some boxes in his bedroom, Jean found a receipt for a hotel in Santa Barbara made out to Mr. and Mrs. Wilkinson on a date when she was nowhere near Santa Barbara. Then there was another receipt for a liposuction procedure—and she knew neither of them had had that! And so began the feelings of betrayal and anger. "Once I could let go of the anger, I actually felt free," Jean said. "In retrospect, I think I didn't want to know. He gave me almost everything I wanted, except loyalty."

When asked what is she most proud of looking back on her life, she quickly replies, "My kids." What would she do differently if she could? "Not have an open marriage!" And how about advice for young women starting out today? **"Be true to your feelings. Honor how you feel. If you feel sad and someone tells you not to be, don't listen to them."**

What's next for Jean Wilkinson? "I'm planning my ninetieth birthday party next month," she smiles. "I give good parties. I'm having a caricaturist and a cake with my picture on it." And just as I'm about to put away my pen and paper, she adds, "Oh, and I can't wait for my *Vanity Fair* magazine to arrive. It has eighteen pages of Caitlyn Jenner. He was a gorgeous man, and now she's a beautiful woman. She'll do a lot of good for people."

Read as much as you can.

Isabel Arteaga | 1904
Mexico City, Mexico
Died: 2003

*Tu pleures tes mortes, mais tu
ne t'enterres pas avec eux.*
Cry when people die, but don't
bury yourself with them.

Aline Lavergne Tanguay | 1925
Buckingham, Canada
Died: 1995

It's better to have a birthday
than **NOT** to have a birthday.

Mitzi Webber | March 5, 1931
Rancho Mirage, California

Nina Shildneck | February 21, 1935
Boulder, Colorado

How you feel is an attitude. You can choose to feel good no matter what or you can choose to feel bad no matter what. Despite a lot of health problems, I'm a happy person because I choose to be. And peer groups are important. These are the people who have shared history with you.

Patricia Jeannie Verlander | November 30, 1933
Oakland, California

One of the most important things I learned the hard way is to forgive and be a truly good and caring person to all of your friends and family. Be grateful. We take so much for granted. We need to stop and appreciate what we have.

 **Gaillard Lewis** | August 16, 1912
El Paso, Texas
Died: December 4, 2014

I had the pleasure of interviewing Gaillard just weeks before she passed away peacefully in her sleep. At 102 years old, she was sharp as a tack, and gracious and warm with a huge smile, which made her passing all the more shocking when I learned of it. Right up until the end, she was proud of her art and delighted to share it, generously giving me the piece shown to take home.

I was born in El Paso, Texas, but lived most of my life in California. I graduated from UCLA Class of '35 with majors in political science and art. Later I went back and got a Master's degree in silversmithing. For thirty-four years, I taught art in high schools in Pasadena, California. The most vivid memory I have of teaching was taking a group of students to Europe to go to museums and see the art. Right before my eyes, I could see the students change as a result of the experience. I'll never forget that.

It's important to follow your passion, but you still have to have a skill. Art was always my passion. I found a way to make a living with it by teaching art. Teaching was the skill. A woman needs both a profession and a job to survive. Choose a broad field that will give you many choices. Art is like that.
There are many different ways you can go.

Having a wide array of choices is important. You can always specialize in an area you love. When just starting out, you don't have mastery, but if you love something and keep at it, over time you will become a master.

My grandmother told me to "treat your husband like a king." I thought this was old-fashioned and learned the hard way the true meaning of her wisdom. I chose to put my children in front of my husband, and he did not feel how much I valued him. I am now happily remarried and fully understand her wisdom. My husband and I put each other first as a king and a queen.

Marjorie Elliott

April 28, 1909
New Ross, Nova Scotia
Died: March 10, 1997

Be happy with the life and hand you
are dealt. Don't try to be something
that you aren't. Live simply.

Betty Cormack | August 24, 1929
Deniliquin, NSW, Australia

Don't hesitate to go to a party because you don't
have a new dress or think you won't have fun.
It could be the party you enjoy the most!

Virtudes Blanco de Yurre | March 26, 1908
Pinar del Rio, Cuba
Died: May 28, 2007

Advice to artist Synthia Saint James on how to manage the nervousness associated with public recognition:

First, don't even think about it. Don't forget to say thank you. But most of all, always remain humble.

Lena Horne | June 30, 1917
Brooklyn, New York
Died: May 9, 2010

Make sure you take care of your body, live a clean, wholesome life, and use your brain to get what you want, not your body. My husband married me for who I was, not my body, and we were married for fifty-eight years.

Lucy P. Virdure | May 3, 1924
Port Allen, Louisiana

Don't ever trust a guy more than 50 percent.

Kimberly Song | November 9, 1939
North Korea

A favorite line from a song reminded me to let go of toxic people: "I didn't give a damn for any man who didn't give a damn for me."

Edith Purville | October 6, 1908
White Plains, New York
Died: 2004

Jean Bruce Poole | July 13, 1924
London, England

If you think a woman in her nineties would be easy to schedule an interview with, think again. Jean Bruce Poole keeps a calendar that would put people five decades younger to shame. When she's not at her yoga class, she's taking a workshop on how to be a lay counselor in her church or sitting on the planning committee for a new independent living community. What was scheduled as an hour-long interview turned into two hours as Jean shared the real secrets of a long, healthy, and happy life.

My motto is to keep going. A good diet and exercise makes a difference. Today I'm taking two yoga classes. I normally wouldn't put them on the same day, but I like this one instructor. She has us exercise in a chair. You'd be surprised how much energy you can use sitting in a chair using weights.

Growing up in England, I remember waiting for the war to happen. I was about twelve. We listened to the news every night at six o'clock, and it was more and more horrible and frightening. Then they started building air raid shelters in Hyde Park. We all thought when war came that it would be the end of everything. My parents were worried because they thought Chamberlain* was terribly mistaken. When he came back from Berlin saying "peace in our time," we were really very upset and worried. Then in 1939 when war was declared, nothing happened. We were all issued gas masks, which we never used. My school was evacuated from London and we went to Buckinghamshire where we were billeted in another school. There was a bomb that went off close to our home at Brucefield when Churchill came to stay nearby. The bomb landed about a half mile from the house and created a huge crater that's still there today.

The bombing of London came later and I was there. I graduated from high school in Manchester. My aunt and I, with whom I was staying, went to visit with a friend of hers and when we came back her house had been bombed. I actually spent the night in Manchester prison. Not in a jail cell, but in a room there. Then I was sent to stay with some friends. That part of the war was not very happy for me.

My eighteenth birthday was in July 1942, and in August I joined the WRNs.** Everyone was doing something to help the war cause so it seemed like the right thing to do. My job as a Wren was as a plotter. We plotted shipping with radar points from stations along the coast. It gave us blips on their machines. It was a brand-new technology. I had the choice of doing Station X, which was where they did the secret codes, but I decided I didn't want to work with numbers. If I had gone to the secret codes I would have been working with Alan Turing.*** My father knew and liked Turing.

After the war, I went to France to study French civilization and the French. I studied at the Sorbonne. It was while I was there, in November 1949, that I married my first husband. He got a job with the Marshall Plan**** and we lived in Paris for a while, but he was originally from Pasadena, California, and when we left Paris that's where we went. I love the French and I love Paris. I met Julia Child through her sister, Dort. They were from Pasadena, too. I went to the Cordon Bleu with Julia once. They were making beef kidneys. I haven't tried it too often since, but they were actually very good. Julia was very nice, lovely. And her husband, Paul, was really fun and interesting. I really enjoyed them.

We moved to Pasadena in 1952 when my youngest was seven months old. It was challenging. Compared to Paris, I thought it was a small town. What made things much better was that people were very kind. I got involved in the Junior League. A nice friend of the family proposed me as a member and I joined. I ended up being different committee chairs. And then, the most fun of all was becoming a docent at the Huntington Art Gallery in 1958. The art curator was fabulous.

In 1977 I decided I wanted a divorce. Let's just say it was due to irreconcilable differences. A priest from the church I went to who was helping me told me he thought I should do it. Here I was, struggling all along, and it was an unbelievable relief to have so-called sanction from the church. I never looked back. It was so much better.

I had to go to work. I had three children by now. It was kind of wonderful. A friend told me about a job at the Old Mill in San Marino. It's a mill that was built in 1816. El Molino Viejo. I went to work for the Southern California Historical Society. I did things like put up panels and exhibits and organized events. I would go to San Francisco for meetings of the board. I enjoyed it. It was interesting. I learned a lot there.

After five years at the Old Mill, I went to work at El Pueblo in downtown Los Angeles as senior curator. In fact I wrote a book about it, *El Pueblo: The Historic Heart of Downtown*. One of the things I'm most proud of is preserving the David Alfaro Siqueiros' mural painted in 1932. A previous director of the Pueblo thought the mural was subversive and she ordered it to be whitewashed. When I came to work, it was somewhat coming through, and I realized it was something important. I convinced our boss to let us start a Save the Siqueiros committee.

I've been married twice since my divorce. My second husband died in 1995 of esophageal problems. I met him when I was working on the Pasadena Centennial.

We were going to have a ball to celebrate it. I asked a friend if she could help me and if she could find someone for me to go to the ball with. We were married for twenty-one years also. My third husband I met at a party. We were married for nine years, and he died in 2012. By then I was too old to change my name, so I just kept my second husband's name.

My life, it hasn't been about just keeping busy. It's about being stimulated. Being curious and wanting to know about things. I'm a bit leery of giving advice to people. In our lay counseling class, I learned that we're not there to give advice but to understand what the issues are, discuss what possible solutions there might be, and help people come to them. One thing I know to be true after all of my years of living, is that **a drop of honey is a lot better than a drop of vinegar.**

Author's Notes:
* Neville Chamberlain was British Prime Minister when England entered World War II. He was known for his policy of "appeasement" toward Nazi Germany.

**The Women's Royal Naval Service (WRNs) was first formed in 1917 during World War I and disbanded in 1919. The group was then resurrected in 1939 at the beginning of World War II. The women performed the roles of cooks, clerks, wireless telegraphists, radar plotters, weapons analysts, range assessors, electricians, and air mechanics.

***Alan Turing is widely considered to be the father of theoretical computer science and artificial intelligence. A movie about his life, *The Imitation Game*, was released in 2014.

****The Marshall Plan was an American Initiative to help countries in Western Europe rebuild after World War II.

Life . . . you take it for what comes. If it comes happy, you're happy. If it doesn't, you let it roll right off your shoulders. I have no regrets. All my life I believed that if you have a job to do, you do it. It doesn't matter whether you like it or not. It's just there. You do it. I'm not afraid to die. When the man upstairs is ready for me, I'm ready for Him.

Marjorie H. Wall | October 24, 1922
Merriam, Indiana
Died: April 21, 2015

Stay in school and get an advanced degree in a specialty area. Specialize, specialize, specialize. The narrower the focus, the more successful you will be.

Peggy Covell | June 27, 1940
New York, New York

Before you get married, get your man drunk to make sure he's a happy drunk and not abusive. Do this before you say YES!

Joann Gernert | August 5, 1925
Phoenix, Arizona

Eileen Hutchings
July 26, 1924
Willow Lake, South Dakota

I was born on a farm. Looking back, I had a great life. Before the Depression started in 1929 and then the drought in 1930, I lived in a big farm house with barns, pighouses, and lots of animals. Every morning I gathered eggs. I had four brothers who were between ten to twenty years older than me. When I was born my brothers thought, "Mom and Dad still do that stuff?" Once I started growing up they intereacted with me, but it was more like being an only child.

My father had leased the land to buy more land, so when the Depression and drought hit he lost everything. No one else had the money to buy the farm, so we lived there for a while until my parents found a smaller farm near town. I wouldn't want to live on a farm now, but it gave me an appreciation of the outdoors. I can remember my mother and her best friend, Fanny, who was also losing her farm, hugging each other and crying in the dining room. I can still picture it. The place we moved to had no electric lights, just kerosene lamps. I learned to value whatever you have, to take care of it, appreciate it, and keep it.

I went to business college and got a job at the State Standard Oil Office. I had to find a place to live and wound up renting a room from my parent's friends, Fred and Fanny. They had a daughter who was also named Fanny. We called them Big Fanny and Little Fanny. This was during World War II. Little Fanny had a boyfriend with a close-knit family that would get together for dinner every Sunday. One day she asked her boyfriend's mother if she could invite me.

We were all sitting at the dining room table, when in walks this handsome guy. He had been in the service and then gone on to college, so I hadn't met him before. We started dating, and about a year later he said he was going to California to go to school, and would I join him and get married? I had never traveled anywhere. It was sad for my parents to see me leave. I quit my job and arranged for the train trip West. His mother decided to accompany me and we had a great time on the train trip. When we arrived, I stayed with his sister at first, then rented my own place. In those days, you didn't live together, so we both rented our own places.

I found a job working at H. J. Heinz in Los Angeles as secretary to one of the managers. I was so naive. One of the managers offered to drive me home because I had to take the bus. He tried to come in with me. We didn't know anyone. The people who owned the house behind where I was living had a son who was a minister. In 1949 he married us in front of their fireplace on a Friday. In 1951 my first daughter was born.

We were living in little apartments over garages in Burbank. Then my husband found a house in West Covina, California. It was a tract home. We still had no car, so we had to take the bus everywhere. His sister lived in Pomona with her three kids, and she would let us use her car when we needed to. Because it was a new neighborhood and everyone had kids, we all became friends. We had a strong sense of community that kept me engaged and having a good time. After being in South Dakota, it was freedom!

One of my dearest friends, Ruth, lived across the street. For years before my husband and I moved away, Ruth and I would meet between her house and mine and spend hours at Polly's Pies. Now she lives too far away and can't drive. It's been six years. It feels sad because we always had such fun together.

When the kids got older, I went to work in my husband's court reporting business. He didn't want me making friends with the employees, and at one point I had no friends. So I worked hard to re-engage with friends from the past. I still have friends in South Dakota.
With new people, you lose them sooner. They move or pass away.

It was a startling day when my daughter Martha called me and her sister, Molly, and said she wanted to talk to us. When we got together, she said she was dating, but not dating boys. Driving home from that meeting, I looked at Molly and said, "What do we do now?"

In thinking about it, I figured this is just the way we live now, and I love my daughter and I want to stay friends with her. It didn't seem awful, but I was thinking, *Well, she was married to two men. How does all this work?* Within a week after she spoke with us and I had thought about it, there was no more discussion. I didn't think anything was wrong with it. I just didn't understand. My concern was telling friends when they asked about Martha and what was happening with the family, and I hoped they would accept it. I wondered how Ruth was going to react. I didn't want to lose any of my friends,

but I knew if they didn't approve they would be gone. Turns out everyone was okay. The only person who reacted negatively was the tailor. When she asked how Martha was, I told her. She told me her brother had married a man, but she didn't go to the wedding because she didn't think it was right. I told her I thought it was fine, and she got kind of bristly with me. Things are pretty much back to normal now with her.

After all of these years of living, what do you know to be incontrovertibly true?
Be nice. People like you better.

Advice to women staying home with kids:
Find some kind of club to make friends. You need people as a support system. It's hard to be alone.

What's the hardest thing about aging?
Not feeling so secure. You have to be financially prepared and not expect someone to take care of you. But you can ask for help. As you get older you do need help and advice. Times change and you have to keep up with it. Hearing is important—get good hearing aids. I got a pair and didn't tell anyone—not even my husband. I just went and got them. When I went to work, everything was so loud! Then I came home and the refrigerator was loud like an engine! So I returned them and put up with being hard of hearing. Then one day, Martha and Molly said they had to talk to me. I thought they were going to tell me I had dementia. They told me I needed hearing aids! I can't believe I'm ninety-one years old. That's getting old. I was so happy when I passed my driver's test at ninety and got my license extended until I'm ninety-five!

**Don't wait for tomorrow to enjoy life. Make an effort
to find time today to do things you like.**

Valentyna Vlasyuk | October 10, 1935
Ostroh, Ukraine
Died: June 18, 2010

Do your best to look your best.

Barbara Hayes | May 22, 1932
Atlanta, Georgia
Died: September 29, 2013

**Do a good deed and throw it in the flowing river,
never expecting anything in return.**

Zare Nadzharyan | January 20, 1928
Tbilisi, Republic of Georgia
Died: August 24, 2013

**Be proud of yourself. You are not a nobody.
You are somebody. Never see yourself as inferior to others.**

Bessie Quinto | Haines, Alaska
Died: February 1967

Love yourself first before you love anyone else.

Lily Bertha | 1874
Ohio
Died: 1905

Know YOURSELF before you get involved with a man.

Martha French | July 29, 1935
Allegan County, Michigan

Abby Root

February 25, 1926
Los Angeles, California

I met Abby in a group of four diverse women who gathered to speak with me at an independent living home in Pasadena, California. She was by far the most reserved of the women, waiting patiently to speak or to be invited to speak. I could see how that patience served her well as a first grade teacher and, later, as a librarian and museum docent with school groups.

I wouldn't do a thing differently. I've had the chance to see my children grow. To be with my husband when he died. Opportunities to discover how incredibly rich the life I'm leading now and getting to know new people and treasure people I've known. The greatest challenge at this stage of life has been being willing to leave a community of friends and embrace a new community.

I went to Reed College in Portland, Oregon, and got a master's from Columbia University in New York. I taught first grade at private schools, then taught in Denver, Colorado. Once I had a child and a father-in-law to care for at home, I became a librarian because there was no "homework" involved. It was a strategic move that enabled me to work and meet my family responsibilities. When I retired, I taught in Nagasaki, Japan, for two years in a girl's school. It was the only city open to the West at the time from 1987 to 1989.

When we came back from Japan I wondered what I would do with the rest of my life. I saw a museum needed a docent for school groups that went through on Mondays and I did that for almost twenty years. It was a teaching museum so I got to use my skills from my career. I only left because I wanted to move to be nearer my family.

There's always something to be amazed at every day. You may not know what it is when you get up in the morning, but there will be something to astonish you. People and nature offer continual delights.

I can never
remember a name
but I can always
forget a face.

Joy Simonson | 1919
Washington, D.C.
Died: 2007

Treat people the way that you
would want to be treated.

Inez Curry | April 1, 1920
Shaw, Mississippi
Died: February 8, 2011

If you don't have nothing nice
to say, don't say it all at.

Elizabeth Faustine | October 15, 1911
Bridgeport, Connecticut
Died: 2006

Dr. Judy Rosener | November 9, 1929
Los Angeles, California

At eighty-six years old, Dr. Judy Rosener continues to be a force to be reckoned with. Always ahead of her time, Judy wrote about women and leadership for the Harvard Business Review *over two decades ago before it was on anyone's radar screen. Ask her a question and she will take you down a winding path from one thought to the next, each intertwined, and to follow her you must pay close attention. Otherwise, she will dance rings around you and leave you in her verbal dust. With Judy, if you snooze, you lose. She admits that her body is moving slower these days, but in speaking with her, it's clear that her mind is as nimble as ever.*

I've had a great life. I was born during the Depression, to a large, loving, poor, but well-educated family. I've been happily married for sixty-four years, I'm the mother of three and widely traveled children. Unexpectedly, I've had a career as professor at UC Irvine, an author, and a speaker. I never planned any of this. How did it happen? In part I attribute it to serendipity.

My undergraduate degree is in sociology from UCLA. I got married, then I got bored. My cousin invited me to a party in Irvine just when the University of California, Irvine was getting started. I decided to go back and get a master's degree, then I earned my PhD at age fifty. After that, I wound up working at UC Irvine for thirty years as a professor teaching business and government, and later diversity.

In 2011 I did a TED Talk on Serendipity. Everything is connections. Planning can be a mistake because you wind up going where you think you should go.

Community colleges are good for this reason. They enable you to explore first. To get to serendipity you have to be open. Talk to everyone you meet. I met someone in an airport who later introduced me to Hillary Clinton and now we're friends. One of my daughter's paintings hangs in the Clinton home.

Having female friends is also really important. Men build relationships based on what they do together. Women build relationships by understanding one another. For example, my husband plays tennis with a man named Frank. When I ask him what Frank's last name is, he says he doesn't know. When I ask what Frank does, he doesn't know that either. "I just play tennis with him," my husband says. Women show an interest in each other.

If you're not on the edge (taking chances), you're taking up too much space. However, to be on the edge, you need to feel good about yourself, because when you feel good about yourself, so will others. Most important, when you're on the edge, serendipity takes place—you experience important, unexpected opportunities that occur by accident.

An exciting and fulfilling life is about serendipity; living on the edge, and exposing oneself to unexpected and unplanned opportunities. This requires taking personal and professional risks which often lead to unanticipated personal and professional options. Make lots of friends and connections because you never know where they will lead and/or support you.

Always smile at people
when you walk by them on
the street. It doesn't cost
you anything and people
want to be seen.

Sonia Frankel | May 21, 1925
Perth Amboy, New Jersey
Died: August 16, 1995

My mother hocked and hocked about education. She felt the only way you could have a life was through education. She worked hard her whole life and it didn't bother her but she never made friends because she was always working.

Frances Levenson | 1901
Perth Amboy, New Jersey
Died: 1962

It's never too late
to start your day.

Irene F. Lee | August 3, 1926
Manorville, New York
Died: August 4, 2014

Esse quam videri.
To be, rather than to seem.

Elaine Weinberg | April 7, 1929
Newport Beach, California

First get married then have children. That's what I did and I had the happiest life.

Thelma Verbeck | August 7, 1925
New Orleans, Louisiana

I've been married 70 years and the secret is to never be jealous of your husband. Trust one another and support one another. And remember that family always comes first.

Symbol Winkie Ordeneaux | February 3, 1925
Gramercy, Louisiana

If you don't want
to do something,
simply say no!

Beverly Braman | April 29, 1933
Westborough, Massachusetts

Nelly Galafassi DaRosso

January 11, 1929
Le Quesnoy, Nord-Pas-de-Calai, France

Chi ha tempo non aspetti tempo.

This phrase came into my mind earlier this year as I was driving to the hospital. Mario, my husband of sixty-five years, had recently been diagnosed with stage four lung cancer. The simple Italian phrase means **lost time is never found again; do not postpone what you can do now.** This way of life was something my husband and I lived by.

My childhood in Northern France was, at first, idyllic. Then came World War II and the enemy occupied my beautiful fortified town of Le Quesnoy. In fear of our safety, my family fled to Toppo in Northern Italy where my parents grew up. Adapting to a new life and language, I was a young foreigner living in Italy during the most turbulent time in Europe. I dressed differently, spoke another language, and was unknown in my new town. All of which resulted in, for a brief time, being questioned as a spy.

Although Mario had left Toppo before I arrived, his journey was similar. While his father moved to America, Mario spent much of his childhood in Italy with his devoted mother and grandmother. As a teenager, he and the rest of his family moved to America to be with his father. Honoring his new country, Mario joined the United States Army as an Italian Interpreter during the war. He journeyed back to Italy as a soldier and

an American citizen, though his trip was brief due to an explosive device near Cassino, Italy. The explosion seriously injured Mario and his compatriots, resulting in a Purple Heart in honor of his service. After a long period of recovery, Mario came to Toppo to see his grandmother. There, we met soon after his arrival.

In 1950 we married in Italy and settled in Pittsburgh, Pennsylvania. My husband was in the tile business and I raised our two children, Robert and Nancy. As a couple, and later as a family, we always found ways to live for the moment. We enjoyed whatever life had to offer and exposed our children to culture and education. We traveled as often as we could and spent almost every day together. After all of our early life experiences we always looked for positive ways to live.

Mario passed away on April 9, 2015. There is not a day, sometimes not a minute, that goes by that I do not think of Mario. When I think about our life I have some small regrets. He loved the leftover batter in the bowl when I made a cake. Perhaps I should have been less concerned with the cake and left him a little extra batter to enjoy. However, I do not regret the life that we lived and how we lived it. Every day was an adventure . . . our adventure.
We lived *chi ha tempo non aspetti tempo*.

Don't go to bed with your makeup on.
Stay out of the sun so you don't
get all wrinkled. Stop talking
on the other people and look at
yourself. Pray every night. Don't
drink. Don't smoke. Love on your man.
Have enough sex so you can read the
newspaper through
your partner's ear.

Annie Mae Shexnayder Lange | August 19, 1927
Kaplan, Louisiana

78

Grace Jamentz | June, 1926
New Rochelle, New York

At ninety years old, Grace Jamentz has the energy, curiosity, and sense of humor often missing in women many decades younger. She still drives, meets with friends at social events, and generously supports community causes in which she believes.

I was born into an Armenian family. They thought education was very important so I went to Simmons College and graduated from there. Before I met my husband, I worked in New York City in retail sales. I especially loved selling jewelry and antiques. Then I moved with him to Pasadena, California, in 1960. This is where I've lived ever since and I raised my two daughters here.

I describe myself as a "Residential Executive." Working at home is a job. It's working. You have to have skills in psychology, engineering, accounting, time management, and so on. I also say that the library is the "American University." The doors are open to everyone regardless of status. You just have to be curious and learn. It never goes to waste. I can talk to anyone about anything because I have knowledge from reading so much on such a wide variety of topics.

The advice I would give to young women today is:

◎ **Make friends and keep making them. They will die, leave, and you'll still have a support system if you continually make friends.**

◎ **Don't focus on age. Focus on what you have yet to do.**

◎ **Don't focus on your limitations; focus on your strengths. You may not be good at sports, but you're good at other things.**

◎ **Don't be afraid to say what everyone else is thinking. They'll appreciate you for it. Especially if you can say it in an inoffensive way.**

 November 21, 1913
Denton County, Texas

I was born on a farm to a father who was a sharecropper. In 1943 I joined the Women's Army Corps. We were given some of the benefits that the men got, but not all. I worked as the Message Center Chief in Naples, Italy, at the supply depot, then I was moved to Livorno, Italy, when the front moved North. When I went into the service I was already married and we both thought it would be better to be inside than to be living on the outside with things being rationed. In the service we got fifty dollars a month with room and board, which wasn't bad. I also joined because I wanted to help end the war. Someone had to do it. Besides that, it was a chance to go overseas.

Men would complain because women were taking the desk jobs, which meant they had to go out and do manual labor. Four hundred thousand women joined the service during World War II. I spent my thirtieth birthday at sea going from Newport News, Virginia, to Casablanca, Morocco. My husband and I were serious about winning the war. When we returned we moved to Oak Ridge, Tennessee, I continued to do office work and raised our daughter alone after my husband died. The people working in Oak Ridge didn't know it at the time, but they were working on the atomic bomb.*

The advice I would give a young woman today is trust in the Lord and he will direct your ways.

*Author's Note: Oak Ridge is the home of the "Manhattan Project" that developed the first atomic bomb dropped on Hiroshima, Japan, on August 6, 1945. It consisted of more than sixty thousand acres and housed tens of thousands of workers and their families. The complex was entirely sur-rounded by walls with armed guards stationed at all entry points. The project was shrouded in so much secrecy that most workers had no idea what they were doing.

"Can't" never did anything.

Vernice Kussmaul | May 22, 1920
Los Angeles, California
Died: June 30, 2005

Never lose your sense of humor.

Annette Stormant | April 30, 1942
Toledo, Ohio

Where there's a will, there are ten to fifteen different ways!

Daisy Chambers | December 1, 1929
St. Louis, Missouri

Do not regret
growing older.
It is a privilege
denied to many.

Eleanor Scotty Leonard | May 8, 1932
Scotland

In a painful and cruel twist of irony, a high school junior wrote a report about her great-grandmother that ended with, "I'm happy that I did this report because now I have something concrete to someday show my children." But Quimby Rae Ghilotti, a popular student at Napa High School, will never have children to share it with—she was killed eighteen months later in the collapse of a waterslide at a local amusement park. This excerpt honors both the author of that report and its subject.

A Personal Family History

by Quimby Rae Ghilotti

No one is quite positive of the exact date of my great-grandmother's arrival in America. We think it was 1897. Her name was Adelina Malina Sjogen. She was born in Gottenberg, Sweden, in 1883. At the age of fourteen she boarded a boat by herself and headed for America. The boat was cold and the sleeping bunks had only eighteen inches between each bunk. She was alone, cold, and terribly frightened. Her only possessions were a small basket of food to last her the entire trip and a few pieces of clothing. The boat landed in New York and from there she took the train to Oakland, California, in search of her older sister, Sophie, who was twenty years old.

The Sjogen family first sent Sophie to America, as other Swedish families did, in hopes of her finding a better life. The living conditions and opportunities were much better than in Sweden. Sophie loved America. The people were kind and friendly to her. Surprisingly, there were no stereotypes against them. She worked as a housekeeper and eventually sent for her sister, Adelina. When they found one another in the United States, Adelina and Sophie had a joyous reunion.

Adelina stayed with her sister until she found a job of her own. They were both very happy to have such wonderful opportunities and to be together. However, they missed their parents and their last sister who stayed behind in Sweden to take care of them. Both Sophie and Adelina felt bad and guilty about their sister, who had given up the opportunity of a lifetime.

Adelina found a job in Palo Alto. She went to work in the home of a man she called "Old Man Standford" as a housekeeper. My mother fondly remembers her grandmother speaking of him.

According to her, his dream was to open a college right there in America so that American students wouldn't have to travel to Europe for a college education. She admired that greatly in him.

While working for Leland Stanford, Adelina met her future husband, twenty-year-old August Nielsson, who had also come to America from Sweden. He later changed his name to Nelson because it was easier to spell. August and Adelina fell in love, but she had to move to San Jose for a better job while he stayed in Palo Alto. They would save up their money and make trips back and forth to see one another.

On September 28, 1897, Adelina and August were married. Together they purchased a ranch in San Jose. August had finally saved enough money to move and make a family and a home. On the ranch they raised apricots, prunes, and walnuts—as well as seven children. With a thriving business, they could afford to take their children to Sweden to visit their families. It was very special for them to be able to return to the land of their birth with their family.

Adelina passed down many Swedish traditions. One example is the celebration of Santa Lucia Day. This is a Swedish holiday in December. The children in the family leave a pair of their shoes out, and then in the middle of the night Santa Lucia comes and leaves a present in the shoes. The next morning, the oldest daughter makes her parents breakfast and takes it to them wearing a beautiful dress and a halo of candles.

I really wish I knew more about my Swedish relatives. Maybe someday someone will come up with some more information. I hope that is the case! Until then I am proud to be Swedish and hold that name with high esteem.

On going to the doctor:
Don't look and you won't find!

Dorothy Smith | June 19, 1907
Perth Amboy, New Jersey
Died: January 15, 2001

Yesterday is history,
tomorrow is a mystery,
today is a gift . . . the present.
Life is a pilgrimage and
death a return home.

Sister Anne Marie Snyder | February 25, 1923
Cleveland, Ohio

It's important for older people to associate with younger people. They keep you up to date in the world. Otherwise, you become boring and caught up in your aches and pains. It's not that you shouldn't have older friends, but make sure they have remained vital. There's a world outside of you. It may not always be great, but it's our world.

Doris Dorie Snedeker | December 16, 1924
Lakewood, Ohio

If you are feeling depressed, open a newspaper and read it end to end and you'll realize your problems are small compared to other people's problems.

Beda Perez

May 27, 1932
Falfurrias, Texas
Died: October 10, 1987

Never talk back to your mother or she'll break your teeth.

Paula Coro | 1910
San Jose Punula, Guatemala

Just because
I'm fat and gray
doesn't mean
I'm stupid.

Bobbie Spano | November 6, 1928
Bogalusa, Louisiana

Dr. Rosita Worl | April 29, 1937
Juneau, Alaska

Dr. Worl is the president of the Sealaska Heritage Institute, which is dedicated to preserving and maintaining the Tlingit, Haida, and Tsimshian cultures and language. Her inspiring story reminds us that strength comes from adversity.

Author's Note: From 1921 to 1960, Haines House served as a "home" for orphans, wards of the court, and children from remote villages where schools were not available. In reality, children like Rosita were removed from loving homes by missionaries intent on exposing them to Christianity and non-Native culture.

I was born in a cabin on a beach without a doctor present and raised in Southeast Alaska in a fishing village called Petersberg. My Tlingit names are *Yeidiklats'okw* and *Kaa'hani*, and I'm one of the Ch'áak' (Eagle moiety of the Shangukeidi [Thunderbird] Clan) from the Kawdiyaayi Hít (House Lowered from the Sun) of Klukwan, and a Child of the Sockeye Clan. Our tradition is that one child in the family goes to live with grandparents. I was that one.

They didn't want me to go to school, but social welfare came and took me away to Haines House.* They were taking Native children to educate and "Christianize" them. It was traumatic. I still have vivid memories. The woman who took me asked me if I wanted to see my brother and I said yes, but I didn't realize it meant I had to go away on a plane—and that my brother was just used as an excuse to get me to go with them. He wasn't where we were going. As we drove away, we passed my grandparents, who were working, and when I cried out the social worker told the driver to keep going. I was put in the back of a float plane and I fought to try to get away from them. But I was restrained. I wet my pants. I was only six years old. Haines House was an orphanage—which was ironic because I wasn't an orphan.

I had to learn to really make it on my own at six. I was removed from my whole family. Eventually my grandparents worked something out so that my aunt could work at Haines House. In Clinket style, the off-spring are viewed as brothers and sisters. She was not my biological mother, she was my aunt, and it took her three years to get me out of the home. When she wasn't there I had to learn to fend for myself, and I was always getting in trouble. The good girls would tell me, Why don't you listen? I enjoyed the punishment because they sent me into the field. Sometimes I had to do things to protect myself so that I wasn't punished further. If I wet the bed at night, I'd lie in the urine to soak it up.

When I finally left there, I lived with my Aunt Bessie and she trained me—she must have seen something in me. I went through rigorous training with her. She made me work hard. She taught me how to sit properly and how to hold my head. Aunt Bessie was a union organizer, and at eleven years old I would travel with her and record the minutes of the meetings. In all of her teachings she would tell me I was special. The most important piece of advice I got from her was to be proud of myself. She would tell me, "You are not a nobody. You are somebody. Never see yourself as inferior to others." She imbued that in me so that I had the inner strengths needed to work for our people. She told me I had an obligation to work for our people because of these strengths.

My mother worked for economic equality and civil rights. I remember going to a meeting with her and Governor Gruening. I thought about all she had done, and she became my model. When my mother died the koogeinaa (family banner) was officially passed to me, a symbol that I was to take her place. I was trained from early childhood to work for our people. Now I teach younger people. I focus on the Natives. My mother gave me this teaching that I have a responsibility. And to have knowledge, an education. William Paul introduced me to books. He taught me how to use knowledge to advance ourselves. He was a Native land rights advocate and the leader of the Alaskan Native Brotherhood. I would read his books. He said these are our tools to advocate for our people.

I've learned that you can get angry and mad at people because they dismiss you, but if you advance rational arguments they can't dismiss you. Knowledge is power and influence. I was viewed as a militant during the 1960s. I would see that people would dismiss me if I was angry. But talking with some knowledge was a powerful lesson.

The most important factor in my walk with the Lord is His word. Throughout my years, Scripture has maintained and given me stability. Isaiah 40:10 says: "I do not fear for God is with me and I am not dismayed for I know He is my God and will strengthen and help me and uphold me with His righteous Right Hand." This has been my verse to live by and it has never failed.

Ruth Kisinger | March 7, 1920
Mesa, Arizona

Always hold your head up and walk like you own the state of Texas no matter what is happening in your life. It's important to exude confidence. With the Grace of God and the struggle I made it, so hang in there.

Amanda Bridges | February 9, 1935
Grambling, Louisiana

Suzanne Berger

February 24, 1934
Kimball, Nebraska

> Hang in and don't let people get you down. Don't let anyone crush your spirit. A job to earn a living is a necessity, but you need one you love where you can give and share. Otherwise your light goes out.

When I was little I had bright red hair and freckles. I was what people today would call a nerd. It took me a while to learn to believe in myself. I was high-spirited from being raised on a cattle ranch where I got to roam around free all day. From that I developed a free spirit. High school and college were good, but they took away my sense of freedom. My first marriage was abusive. I was in that marriage for twenty-one years and I had three kids. The kids are the reason why I stayed, but looking back I could have left with the kids and everything would have been okay. I had a degree as a lab tech and could have easily gotten a job. But my confidence was worn down from the abuse.

Once I got out, I saw that the world is much bigger than the confines of being a housewife. Sometimes I'm angry for allowing myself to be repressed and sublimated. I wasn't physically abused, but sometimes I wish he had hit me so that I would have left sooner. The night before I left, I was threatened with a pistol. The next morning I called Bekins, packed up the kids, and moved to a furnished apartment. It all happened within a day. I had the plan in place in my head.

People are led to believe that they have to get married and have children. There's a stigma even today about not choosing that life. I always wanted a job. Getting married was totally socially expected. I had my degree and you think you can always get out, but social pressure causes you to stay. Organized religion is a locus of power no matter how progressive you think you are. Jesus was just one of many Jewish preachers. He was beat up. The church was always one place where you were whole and accepted—it's easy to get caught up in the doctrine when it's really the comfort you want. Your soul is sacred regardless of organized religion telling you who you should be.

Believe in your dreams, hold fast to them, and make them come true.

Anita Milz | August 8, 1931
Zurich, Switzerland

Virginia Havens | October 13, 1925 / Cleveland, Ohio

Life is better if you choose to be positive. This means choosing solutions and seeing what's possible. Learn from your mistakes. If you don't make mistakes, you don't have the opportunity to learn. **Nervousness comes from not wanting to become an adult. To be a full-blown adult, you have to have confidence. Moving into being an adult is so freeing. I'm not afraid of anything now.**

It's wonderful to arrive at this age and not feel scared, handicapped, or restrained. I can do anything or be anything. One of the guiding principles of my life I remember hearing when I was a young woman is: **if I had but two loaves of bread, I would sell one and use the money to buy hyacinths for the soul.** Traveling along the path of life, trust the world. So many people see the world as dangerous. Two or three times I almost died, but something surged up in me to survive. I'm going to Paris to celebrate my ninetieth birthday because it's the most beautiful city in the world and it holds so many wonderful memories.

Eileen Mershart | December 16, 1944 / Chicago, Illinois

It's important to listen to your inner voice about things. And sometimes that's a difficult thing to do. Happiness really is an inside job but it's made difficult because of societal pressure to conform to certain things. Peer pressure, expectations, messages from the media—all push women and girls into areas that in their hearts they don't really want to do.

There are role models today who speak volumes to women about doing what they want to do. Rachel Carson and Jane Goodall were models for me. Women in the political world and in science, medicine, and technology all open up avenues for women. Teachers have a huge role in this. Teachers need to make sure that classrooms are open to ideas and that all ideas are welcome. Classrooms are international marketplaces for breaking down barriers and tickling people's curiosity about what they can do.

To better access that inside voice, young women should observe the world and question attitudes and expectations. Take time to think about it and minimize the noise so that you can actually do that. I hope younger women don't get disillusioned trying to make sense of a crazy world. We've come a long way, but there's so much farther we need to go. There's a lot of noise and rhetoric that doesn't help anything at all.

Don't be discouraged by that. Stay hopeful.

Live each day as if it was your last 'cause one of these days you're going to be right.

Roberta Youtan Kay | November 8, 1943
Los Angeles, California

Minisa Crumbo | 1942 Tulsa, Oklahoma

"The core energetics of the first gift that the Creator bestowed upon us all are the Mother Earth and the Father Sky-Sun. By following the seasons that these ancients weave anew every moment, we encounter the first and most enduring ceremonies of the personal home circle and a schoolhouse of abundant and trustworthy wisdom and knowledge. It is out of our worthy and anguished need, necessity, and desire to connect, merge, and bond with the source of life that we are able to successfully seek, forge, and, ultimately, to partner our own divine format as a co-creator within the format of the Life Force itself."

Excerpt from *Spirit Talk: A Book of Days*
by Minisa Crumbo

I was born in the black-jack hills of Northeast Oklahoma, a member of the Citizen band and Muscogee tribe of Indians. When I was six years old, my family moved to Taos, New Mexico. We lived at the Taos Pueblo Indian School,* homeland of the Taos Homeland Indians. My mother was a teacher there and my father worked in town. Living at the foot of Taos Mountain, I learned to love the Mother Earth and the Father Sky-Sun as my elemental parents. I love them as I love my biological mother and father. I breathe, eat, and live because of all that my elemental parents provide to me.

It's important that we always remember that we are sacred beings and nothing comes between us and the Creator, *Mamogosnan* (Potawatomi language). Be grateful for life however you interpret it. Native Americans don't tell people how to live. Most human beings would like to be told who they are and how to act. The greater part of finding who we are must spring out of our natural wisdom. *Migwech, wewene kiche migwech* = thank you, thank you very, very much.

That is the way we express gratitude for everything in our lives.

I worked with the public for thirty years and founded the Moon Circles Teaching Group, a profound study of what it means to be a woman. The subject of feminine empowerment through biology isn't a topic of discussion in indigenous communities because it's ingrained in us from an early age. No one is seeking empowerment because if your relationship with the Creator is in place and you live in gratitude, that is empowerment. It knows no gender.

My book, *Spirit Talk*, is about the Medicine Wheel Teachings. Although I wrote the book, the teachings are not mine. They are grounded in my experience, but the Creator actually spoke through me. The moment the book was completed, I realized I had achieved my sacred charge and owned my life in a new way. It took me seventy-two years, but I accomplished it.

*Authors Note: Taos Pueblo is the only living Native American community designated as both a World Heritage Site by UNESCO and a National Historic Landmark. The adobe structures are estimated to be over a thousand years old. The homes are generally passed down from one generation to the next with, usually, the eldest son being the sole owner. These homes are still used for religious and cultural activities.

Live a hundred years. Study a hundred years.
Die an idiot anyway.

Katharina Vasilev | October 4, 1922
Sofia, Bulgaria

Put cream on your body because no one else will do it for you! Take care of your body, because no one will do it for you! Don't drink coffee as it will stunt your growth!

Bertha Klein

1878
Budapest, Hungary
Died: 1960

Carol Wilson Floren | September 14, 1935
Freeport, Louisiana

Family is everything. There are so many things you share. Some are happy and others are sad. When no one else is there, your family is.

Dorothy Goldberg | July 26, 1930
Dunkirk, New York

Love is the best thing in the world. My parents loved me. I loved my children. My friends have loved me and I loved my friends. Love has made a life.

THE ADRIAN DOMINICAN SISTERS

In the mid-1970s, a naive young Jewish woman arrived on the campus of Barry College in Miami Shores, Florida. She was to serve as the first dormitory Counselor-in-Residence at this all-girls school run by the Adrian Dominican sisters. There she would build a lifelong friendship that spanned over four decades with one of the sisters who she remembers fondly as young, dark-haired, and always determinedly marching across campus in a white habit and black veil flowing in the wind behind her. The Jewish woman—no longer young and not quite as naive—is me, and my friend, Sister Beverly Bobola, now resides at the Mother House in Adrian, Michigan.

When I asked Sister Beverly if she could arrange for me to speak with some of the sisters for this book, she graciously obliged. I spent an early summer afternoon immersed in the history of this "Order of Preachers," learning from some very special women who have devoted their lives to serving God and the community. Here are parts of their stories and the wisdom they chose to share with me.

Sister Ann Patrice Remkus | July 2, 1928 Rockford, Illinois

I grew up in a small Lithuanian parish. The community was very close knit. There were only five children in the class at Saint Casimir's where a Lithuanian order of sisters ran the school. I learned so much at that school that when I went to high school I didn't learn anything new. I would often stay after school to help the sisters. I did a lot with them. I wanted to be like them. They were young, they had fun with one another, and they treated us with respect.

The high school I went to was run by Adrian Dominicans. I got involved in everything I could. I tried to forget that I was called to religious life. As a teenager I wasn't sure I wanted to do this. I realized it wouldn't be as much fun as it had seemed like it would be when I was a young girl. But I was attracted to the goodness of being a sister. Wanting to be like them was like God was nudging me.

It turned out that the Dominicans were even more fun than the Lithuanians. At seventeen I entered with one friend from high school and together we became postulates with the Adrian Dominicans. Looking back, the greatest challenge I had was leaving my family. The night before I was to say my final vows my mother took me aside. She knew I wasn't sure about my decision. But quickly it became clear that it was the right choice. After spending time at the Mother House, my father said, "I've never seen people who love one another so much." He was impressed with the normalcy of it all.

The best part of being a sister is living with other people who are aiming for the same goal and this being the center of our lives. You realize God is leading us all together toward home. I know for sure that God loves me.

If I could have one do over, I would be a ballet dancer. But I'm too clumsy. I'm always bumping into things. When I reach heaven I hope to hear God say, "Come in at last."

Whatever you do in life you need others, but more than anything you need God. Don't try to do things alone. Individualism promotes fierce competition and lack of discerning for each person's unique gifts. Too much emphasis on money distorts thinking, living, and loving.

Sister Arnold Benedetto | January 19, 1922
Macon, Georgia

During my college years I received a call from God. I was studying at Siena Heights College. We had religion and theology classes. *Vocation* is Latin for *calling*. I didn't want to be called but the sisters encouraged it. My mother objected because she had two priests and one sister in the family already. She wouldn't let me enter until after I got my Master's degree at Catholic University. She said, "If you're going to take a vow of obedience, be obedient to me!" After a semester at CU I wrote home, and my mother could see I was longing to join the order and she agreed.

I professed in 1944, so I've been a sister for seventy-two years. The biggest challenge has been carrying out what we were told to do. We didn't have choices. We were appointed to our roles. We had to be obedient. But I have lived a wonderful spiritual life with wonderful people.

My advice for young women is to have the courage of your convictions. If you have ideals—live up to them. In the end, it's not following the crowd, it's doing what's right. Everyone has a conscience. Live by your standards.

Sister Kathleen Donnelly | October 7, 1921
West Palm Beach, Florida

I always planned to be a nurse like my mother or to do something in sports like my father who was a baseball player. Then in October of my sophomore year of high school at St. Anne's in West Palm Beach, something happened that changed all that. All of the other girls were in the park behind the school eating lunch but I went to the chapel to say the rosary. I remember it was on a Thursday. One of the sisters saw me there. It was the same sister who used to say I would be good on the other side of a desk—in other words, I would make a good teacher.

That week, Mother Gerald came from the Mother House in Adrian, Michigan, and I was told that she needed a companion to accompany her on the trip back. It might have been the same sister who said I would be good on the other side of the desk that suggested I go. So they brought my mother to the school and showed her the postulant's outfit and said she needed to sew one of these for me by Sunday. In reality, Mother Gerald wanted a postulant.

On Sunday we boarded a train and had a lovely private car because she was the Mother General! We stopped in Jacksonville to visit an orphanage and some of Mother Gerald's family, then we went on to Toledo where we were met by a driver who took us to Adrian. I always say it was a Guardian Angel who brought me here. I was put in the places I needed to be at just the right time. I never questioned that this is where I was meant to be. I could have left at any time I wanted to, but I liked it and I had fun with the other postulants.

I took religion, philosophy, and theology to get ready for religious life. When we graduated there was no ceremony but you got a new name. Until the night before, you didn't know what your name would be. You are permitted to submit three names you might like, but the decision is up to the Mother General. The evening before we took our vows, my father talked to Mother Gerald for some time. The next day I was given the name Charles Mary—a combination of my father's and my mother's names. Charles Mary presented a problem for me. When I would show my identification card people would think I had taken someone else's because I didn't look like a Charles! And that's the name I had until 1972 when we were permitted to use our baptismal names.

After getting my certification I was sent to St. Matthew's in Chicago to teach. A sister in the convent had taught us how to teach. While in Chicago I caught pneumonia and they moved me to Detroit, which wasn't much warmer. When I came down with pneumonia a second time the doctor said I might not survive a third bout, and that's when I was sent to Miami Beach to teach at St. Patrick's. I worked in education for sixty years—from the time I was seventeen until the age of seventy-seven—and all but four of those years I was in Florida. Along the way I got my bachelor's degree and a master's

degree in 1957 from Barry College. For thirty-five years, from 1974 to 2009, I was the principal at St. Hugh's in Coconut Grove.

The greatest challenge I've encountered in being a sister is coming back to Adrian and being thrust into living with over two hundred other sisters. I pretty much lived alone when I was a principal, only once did I have two other sisters live with me.

The advice I would give a young woman today is to ask yourself, how do I relate to people?

You have to love being with the people you are working with and working for. You have to have fun, and that won't happen if you don't like the people.

Never underestimate the power of your God-given talents to help others.

Sister Beverly Bobola | August 13, 1940
Hamtramck, Michigan

Stay young and holy. Absolutely love God and you'll be cared for, have someone to talk to, and someone to love. The most important thing is to bring people closer to God.

Sister Maura Phillips | April 25, 1914
Defiance, Ohio
Died: July 26, 2016

Q: Grandma, what card game do you want to play?
A: One where I can win!

Regina Evans | April 9, 1920
Dell Rapids, South Dakota

*To her kids who urge her to eat healthier
and gain five more years of living:*
Well, I'd rather be happy eating all my food
that didn't use to be bad, than to live five
more years and be an old crab. Do you want
a ninety-nine-year-old crab for a mother?

Gloria Akono | July 14, 1921
Preston, Idaho

*To her grandson, when he asked her to take
down the picture of his ex-girlfriend that she
had posted on the refrigerator:*
"No wonder the freezer was so cold!"

Masako Iwanaga | 1918
Isahaya, Japan
Died: 2013

Love within the family and caring for each other is the one thing in life that is constant.

Shirley Nelson | December 25, 1936
Artesia, New Mexico

I would advise one to listen with the same intensity as talking. Look for positive traits in others who annoy you rather than focusing on their irritating behaviors.

Dr. Barbara Lovell | June 22, 1931
Newport Beach, California

Work hard, be self-sufficient, and remember the ten Commandments, Psalm 23, and the Lord's Prayer, and you'll be fine.

Elizabeth Nelson | July 13, 1936
New Rochelle, New York

 December 6, 1932
Tottenville, Staten Island

One of my earliest memories growing up was of my grandmother baking challah on Fridays. I would take it around in my little wagon to my aunts and uncles who lived in the neighborhood. My grandmother's hands were so fast making the noodles and wine for seders. We would take a ferry from Staten Island to Perth Amboy, New Jersey, and pick out a live chicken at one place, then take it across the street to the butcher who would make it kosher for us.

My father had a newspaper route until the Depression. Then he went into the insurance business, but he didn't do so well. During the war he went to work at the shipyard so he wouldn't get drafted. Eventually, he bought a candy store. All of the family worked there to help keep it going after he went back to delivering newspapers.

I was the only one in my family to go to college. I always knew from the time I was a little girl that I wanted to be a teacher. My brother and sister took commercial courses. My sister wound up going to work for Standard Oil in Manhattan. They hired her because our last name was Smith. Back then, they wouldn't hire you if they thought you were Jewish.

I went to Brooklyn College for my undergraduate degree and then went on to get a master's in education. We had no car, so I took the bus to the ferry, then the ferry to Brooklyn, and three trains to Flatbush.

Friends who could afford it rented a room near the college. While going to school, I worked part-time in a dress store on Staten Island and at a hat supply store on 37th Street in Manhattan. It was free to go to college then. You only paid five dollars for registration. I wound up teaching for thirty years all together, with nine years off in the middle to raise my kids. I taught at Mariner's Harbor and a little schoolhouse in Travis on Staten Island.

Every day after eighty is a gift. My husband and I lived in the same house for forty-three years. When he died, I would lie in bed at night and I couldn't turn off the voices. So I got up and cleaned out the house. I realized I had to go on and make a life. The only way to do it is to reach out to other people. You talk to people, meet people. You don't become close, but friendly. I pushed myself. Doing good for others can make your spirits feel better. You have to make it your business to meet people. I joined two organizations because I didn't really know anyone except my neighbors. One was City of Hope and the other was Friends of the Cultural Arts. It keeps me busy, but it isn't really fulfilling. Sitting in a theater with people isn't purposeful. I need something purposeful. I'm working on finding that.

When your kids call, just listen. They don't really want your advice.

Don't compromise
your independence even
if you choose to live
a traditional life.

Maybel "Maybelle" Harbaugh | 1896
Holdridge, Nebraska
Died: 1994

On raising a difficult child:

You know, if I drowned her when she was a baby, I'd be out of prison by now.

Helen Shanahan | February 26, 1922
Red Fork, Oklahoma
Died: May 28, 2008

On humility:

Count yourself. You ain't so many.

Betty Ann Glasgow | October 25, 1927
Mahwah, New Jersey
Died: July 4, 2013

On excuse-making and rationalizing:

If your aunt had balls, she'd be your uncle.

Irene Cochran | 1929
Chester, West Virginia
Died: 2012

On customer service:

I'm not going to beg *and* pay for it, too.

Patsy Betts | March 8, 1927
Greenbelt, Maryland
Died: September 8, 2011

Renee Krushel | May 1, 1926
Bronx, New York

As a kid I had a spiritual experience. I started hearing voices and seeing visions. It was terrifying to go to bed at night. It got me interested in spirituality. I saw hypocrisy in the Church and started looking elsewhere. Now I would describe myself as a mystic.

One thing that I know is true is that we are all one. Quantum mechanics tells us this and my mystical experiences do too. We are all part of an energetic field. Science knows that there is no one unique particle. War is caused because people don't understand this.

The advice I have for young women today is to know yourself. The easiest way to do this is to start meditating. If you know who you are then you know where you want to go. Our consciousness is limited and we open it through meditation. It's not what you do that's important, it's who you are in your heart. Knowing your true self is most important.

Author's Note: Renee is the author of Ascended Masters Speak, *a spiritual self-help book,*
and The Spiritual Evolution of a Mystic.

Jackie Westland | January 15, 1930
Baraboo, Wisconsin

Advice to Young Women:
Be kind. You can't make a mistake that way.

What do you know to be incontrovertibly true?
I believe in a Supreme Being. There are so many
things that happen that can't be explained.
You have to believe in a higher power.

Thoughts on aging:
It all comes down to health. Part of the journey
is not knowing how long we'll live. In the next ten
years we'll be more of a part of our deaths—we'll
have more say in how we die. I told my daughter
I taught you everything I knew about living, now
I have to teach you how to die. I'm not afraid to
die. I'm afraid of how I'm going to get there.

If you had one do over what would it be?
I would ask my Dad for five thousand dollars to invest
and grow.

Be a good listener, give advice only when asked, be good to animals, and treat **ALL** people with kindness and understanding.

Jean Bogen | December 12, 1934
Huntington Beach, California

Rosalie (Rosie) M. Casaus

April 6, 1899
Atequiza, Mexico
Died: April 17, 2005

The following remembrance of yet another life well-lived was submitted by Rosie's loving granddaughter, Desiree Casaus.

Rosie's mother died when she was eleven months old and her father remarried when she was three. Her stepmother was extremely cruel toward her and her brother and sisters. Her oldest sister, Lupe, became the protector and revered sister. At age seven, a botched knee surgery changed her life forever. For the next fourteen years she had to use crutches and undergo five additional surgeries—none were successful. During her childhood, she endured the insensitivity of children calling her "cripple, cripple!" Finally, at age twenty-one, her father brought her to the United States for her last surgery. The doctor was able to straighten her left leg and fuse the knee. This resulted in keeping the leg permanently straight but allowed her to walk without crutches. Though the leg was stiff, thin, and shorter due to the years of poor medical treatment, Rosie was a new lady! Learning to walk on her own two legs (mastered with a confident limp), she became a powerhouse. Rosie made Los Angeles her new home. She learned English, worked as a seamstress, and always sent money back home to her beloved oldest sister, Lupe, in Guadalajara, Mexico.

In the late 1950s, when she was already in her fifties, Rosie met Jacobo. He was dating her sister Mary Lou, but soon realized that Rosie was the real PRIZE!!!! They dated, and for the first time she was doing all the "normal" things that women do with a partner: going out to movies, dances, and dinner. She was content with the casual relationship, but Jake asked her to marry him. She replied, "But, I don't love you!" Undeterred, he showed up with two tickets to New York and took her to St. Patrick's Cathedral where they were married!

Life presents challenges at any given time and age. Rosie's next surprise was in the early 1960s: motherhood. Now in her sixties, she found herself raising two step-grandchildren, eight and ten years old, who had lost their parents. The following years were filled with unwavering dedication, giving, patience, and guidance. She accepted her newfound and unsolicited responsibilities with strength, courage, and commitment. Rosie nurtured, mended, and artfully molded a unique and sustainable family unit. The children grew and went out on their own. Jacobo died in 1983. Rosie, at ninety-three years old, took in her sister Mary Lou and cared for her until Mary Lou passed at ninety-nine years old.

During her life, she broke what she referred to as "this leg" two more times. Each time, determined to regain her walking spot on the path of life, she healed with poise and gratitude. To this day, I can sense the rhythm of her uneven gait as we walked, arm in arm, through miles of adventures. When Rosie was 85 years old we took a ten-day trip to Finland and Russia. At 88 we traveled together to China. At 99 years old we went back to her home town, Guadalajara. Rosie's 100th birthday was celebrated with a hot air balloon ride. An Alaskan cruise marked her 103rd year, and her last trip was a 105th birthday celebration in Guadalajara! All this with a lady with a limp. It was only after her 100th birthday that we used a wheelchair to travel.

Rosie lived out her life in her own home until she passed away at 106 years old. I returned home to stay and care for her but, in truth, Rosie was the one quietly, lovingly, and prayerfully caring for me, the granddaughter she raised from when I was a child. Rosie became the "Princess," and it was the aim of everyone in the family to spoil her as much as she could endure. She remained simple and easy to please, always happiest in "her chair" nestled in the corner of the living room where she observed and noted all the comings and goings. She was a woman of routine, structure, and discipline. EVERY day she got up, bathed (sponge baths except for full showers on Fridays), walked down the hallway reciting her petitions and gratitude to the Sacred Heart, had breakfast, went to her chair, and said the rosary. During the day she would read, crochet gifts, and write out cards and checks to her charities. She and her day caretakers were always working on something! At night, she watched the news, *Jeopardy*, and *Wheel of Fortune* (because "you learn something"), and usually headed off to bed at 9:00 p.m. She often had vivid dreams that she would later recall, like "having tea with the Kennedys" and "being a soldier in full uniform."

Rosalie Casaus was a study in human life and aging. In retrospect and slow motion, you witness all of the stages of life—walking with ease, to using the cane, to pushing the walker, and finally accepting the wheelchair. Blessed with a sharp mind, mental capacity, and a good memory, she was always ready to listen to classical music, enjoy a good story, or laugh at a joke. Though her most difficult task was not feeling like a burden, she continued to exude dignity, respect, and kindness until the very end. A Lady of grand proportions, her spirit is etched in the hearts of all those who knew her.

Random comments and thoughts from Rosie:

- One day you will understand!
- His Guardian Angel is not in the same category. (Her explanation when you just didn't like someone.)
- I like people just because I like them.
- A man's best friend is a dog!

Concept of womanhood:

- First, be a lady, through that one accomplishes knowing how to talk, dress, think, act, and treat people.
- Life has three qualifications: understanding, patience, and love. With these, you can go a long way.
- When you have two bosses, with one you have to fail.
- Education is important.

Eat right and enjoy life.

Edith Marie Williamson | January 15, 1914
Kingsport, Tennessee

Women should be active.
Being passive will never let you
move on in your life and get
where you are meant to be.

Maria Magdalena Pérez Albarrán | June 2, 1915
Michoacán, Mexico
Died: February 20, 2015

Surround yourself with happy
people and you'll be happy too.

Yvonne Joy Dean | February 14, 1926
Stayner, Ontario, Canada
Died: May 8, 2012

You can look back on what used to be or look forward to the future, but the best thing is to live today for we have no promise of tomorrow and yesterday cannot be changed.

Cora Evans | October 28, 1932
Pelzer, South Carolina

Margaret "Peggy" Kennell

September 27, 1924
Ebensburg, Pennsylvania

As I drove up to the Judson Retirement Community in Cleveland, Ohio, I couldn't help but notice a woman marching around the perimeter of the building apparently giving the gardeners instructions for what she wanted to be planted where. A bit later, with the same confidence and energy she uses to serve on the Gardening Committee, she marched in to meet me, extended her hand, and launched into an incredible tale of resilience and survival.

Growing up, my parents lived across the street from each other in Ebensburg, Pennsylvania. They married before my father went off to college. When I was one year old, my father died suddenly of pneumonia. My brother was born shortly after his death. My mother and I lived with her parents, and when my brother was a toddler he went to live with our paternal grandparents, who were still living across the street.

I have so few memories of my mother, but I do remember her playing the piano and harp. My mother remarried several years later and moved to California. My brother and I were told that we were going to live with her as soon as they had a house. It was several months later when I was seven years old that we learned of her death. We were so sad and disappointed. My brother remained with our paternal grandparents and I with our maternal grandparents. We never saw much of each other during our lifetime.

By now, the country was in the Great Depression and my grandfather lost his business and their lovely home.

All five of their children were no longer living at home, so my grandparents and I moved into a small house on the river in Johnstown, Pennsylvania. Then in March of 1936, they came through the town with megaphones telling us that the dam was going to break and we had to head to higher ground. My grandmother told me she couldn't make it. By then, she wasn't well. She told me to go up the hill because the flood in 1889 had killed thousands of people.

I didn't want to leave my grandmother but I did as she told me. When I got to the top of the hill, this man saw me alone and grabbed me. We ran to one house, but they wouldn't let us in. In the distance we saw a light and walked toward it. It turned out to be a gym where people were going. There, a man shined a flashlight in my face and said, "I'll take her." He looked at me and said, "You don't know me but I know you. I'm the minister of the church where you sing in the choir. I remember you sitting in the front row."

The minister kept me for two weeks before my grandfather came to get me. Everything was ruined from the flood. Two weeks later my grandmother died. My grandfather couldn't take care of me. A new chapter of my life began when a great uncle (my grandmother's brother) came to take me to live in a small town in North Central, Pennsylvania. His wife and three children had died of tuberculosis and he had remarried. Unfortunately, his new wife did not want to care for me, so the next five years were not a happy experience for any of us. But luck was with me when

I met a classmate who had the same name as me on the first day at my new school—Margaret Claire. She invited me home to meet her mother that same day. I developed a very close friendship with her and her wonderful family. They included me in their family life and I felt like another daughter. Father Burns gave me away at my wedding in Erie, Pennsylvania, in 1949.

During those five years I spent a few months each summer visiting my great aunt (my grandfather's sister) in Erie, Pennsylvania. She was a social worker who had never married but who had a successful career. She was the Executive Director of the International Institute. She exposed me to the arts, music, opera, theater, books, and travel. I learned so much about many cultures by associating with her staff and meeting people from many countries. She encouraged me to go into nursing. In 1942, I was accepted at the School of Nursing of the Children's Hospital in Boston, Massachusetts. I attended Simmons College for the basic sciences and graduated as a pediatric nurse.

I became a pediatric surgical nurse working in cardiovascular and plastic surgery at the Boston Children's Hospital. It was there that I met a pediatrician, Dr. John H. Kennell. We married in 1949 and moved to Cleveland, Ohio, in 1952. We had three children, five grandchildren, and two great-granddaughters. Later in life I became a Health Educator at the Cleveland Health Education Museum. I have been an avid volunteer in many diverse areas all

my life. I am a lover of nature, gardening, the arts, and sports. My husband John and I traveled to over forty countries and made many friends in the world.

I feel I am a survivor. After what I have been through, I felt I had to develop an attitude of compassion and caring for others. I am so grateful for all the people who came into my life and inspired me, guided me, and enhanced my life. **Be positive, and build trust and respect for yourself and for others. Look for the best in people, have a sense of humor, keep on moving forward, appreciate even the little things in life.** I learned to be responsible for myself and I wanted to be good and important, and I wanted to learn. I wanted to become the best person I could.

And I would say that Peggy Kennell has met all of those goals and more in a life well-lived.

Although no one in the family wanted to acknowledge it, Barbara Arsham knew the cancer that had taken over her body would soon claim her life. This advice was found in a hidden note written on the pages below the top piece of a paper pad and discovered by her daughter, Joy Anzalone, months after her death.

**Dearest Joy,
Always give your best and most—never settle for less.
Love you,
Mom.**

(And there was a smiley face, before smiley faces and emoticons were popular.)

Barbara C. Arsham | May 29, 1930
Toledo, Ohio
Died: July 1, 1981

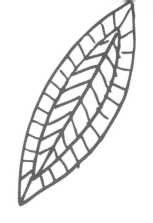

Sometimes for change or progress to take place, death must take place. I used to think that those were harsh words, but this wisdom has been true in my personal, church, and business life!

Mary Gibbs | September 2, 1910
Laurens, South Carolina
Died: September 11, 2001

Hotel Belvedere, located on the shore of Lake Como in Bellagio, Italy, was the vision of one woman who wanted to create a haven for visitors. Since 1880, it has been a family business, lovingly crafted by five generations of women, passed from mother to daughter. Today, three generations of women continue the tradition of warm hospitality: grandmother Signora Lucia, daughter Signora Tiziana, and granddaughter Giulia. I had the opportunity to speak with Signora Lucia, now 88 years old. Although her English is good, her daughter, Signora Tiziana, helped with translation. Theirs is an inspiring story of an enduring passion for, and deep commitment to a family legacy.

My grandmother started The Hotel Belvedere in 1880 as a little trattoria with a bocce ball court. Her husband died, leaving her with five children to support, so she had to do something. My mother was one of those five children. I remember her coming here every day to work. By the time I was born in 1927, it was a hotel with thirty rooms. Now we have seventy rooms. When I was very little and came with her to work, I would play with the children of the groundskeeper who lived in the house next door. I had two brothers and one sister. I was the youngest. When I was seven or eight years old, my job was to prepare the vases with flowers for each table in the dining room. My brother and I would play hotel, where one of us was the guest and the other was the person who greeted him. The game became my reality after I got married in 1954 and came to manage the hotel in 1956.

The biggest challenge in managing the hotel was having to do everything. At one point my sister helped me in reception, but eventually I was the receptionist, the bookkeeper, and helped in the kitchen. I was practically born here so I knew what to do and I kept doing it, but I had to work even harder. There really was no choice. When my husband died, I thought I would have to sell the hotel. I felt like it would be a little too much for my daughter to run, and she didn't really want to. She went to university in Rome, but came back a few months each year to help out. We had to decide what to do. She and her husband came back to help because they knew it was too much for me to run alone. In the end, my daughter wanted to continue the legacy. It was my life, and it was her life. When you live in a place for so long, it's like your home or a child. And all the staff are friends. People are respectful of each other. Now my granddaughter is learning the business. She went to New York to work at the Carlyle Hotel to learn more about the hotel business.

There's nothing else I wish I would have done differently with my life. I was born here and have been happy doing what I did. The best part of the business is meeting new guests and talking with them. I don't like giving advice to others. It's not really helpful unless you see someone in trouble. **People just have to realize that every job has a positive and a negative side, so if you choose to do a job, see the positive. The one thing I know is true after all my years of living is that you are going to work hard all of your life.**

Author's Note: Hotel Belvedere is no ordinary property. The family's commitment to excellence, attention to detail, and emotional investment is evident from the moment you drive up and are greeted like a relative coming for a visit. Interestingly, before I knew it was owned by generations of women, I had thought to myself that a woman surely must be in charge here for everything to be so perfect!

Jeanne Roach | October 4, 1926
Boston, Massachusetts

What's hard about getting older is risk-taking. I would rather live in "happiness." It's traumatic to move in with a group of strangers [at an independent living community]. It's hard to let go of your dreams for your children—and for yourself. You have to hold your goals loosely and be open to other possibilities. You have to approach change as an adventure. I lost two husbands, the first at fifty-two years old. We were very close. I felt like half a person. But I had to go to work—the children were just starting college.

It's important to like what you do. You are going to spend a lot of time doing it. After my first husband died, I discovered who I was. It was a difficult but heady experience to realize I had gifts and capabilities apart from my husband. It's hard for women to embrace the gifts they have. Over the years I found myself volunteering to help make the world a better place. After six months of retirement I said, *I want to go to work to make money.* It was important for me to have value placed on the work I was doing. So I did human resources training, which is a mix of training and mentoring.

What one thing do you know to be incontrovertibly true?

Compassion and love for each other is the ultimate answer. Caring for each other and having empathy. Whatever is happening to one of us is happening to all of us. It's the only thing that will preserve the world.

136

What advice do you have for young women today?

 Make plans to reach your goals but be ready and willing to change course when plans go awry. Think of it as an opportunity to grow.

 Set aside a "Sabbath time" for yourself and keep it sacred. When you're overworked, you're no good to anyone else and a burden to yourself.

 Learn to live with ambiguity. Much of life will fall into that category.

 Tell the truth. Say, "I don't know" when you don't.

 Healthy doses of self-criticism and self-regard are essential.

 Form the habit of not being too attached to things or opinions.

 Don't be afraid to try something new. You might like it. And it makes life richer.

Pick a job you're happy in even if it doesn't pay a lot of money. You'll be happy for the rest of your life. There's always time to have money. Stay home with your children when they're little. It's too soon to go back to work when they're just six or eight weeks old. Children grow up differently when someone other than their parents raises them. Some people can't wait to get the things they want. You can put off getting that new chandelier until you go back to work.

Shirley Rosenblum | July 13, 1922
Tottenville, Staten Island

In typical Midwest fashion, Ella took a little while to warm up during the interview, but once she did she was just a hoot. Her story reminds us that even when you are no longer young, you can find love (or love finds you) in some of the most unusual ways.

My advice for young women is to get as much education as possible. That's what helps you to become independent in times of need.

Dr. Ella Kick | December 14, 1930
Wooster, Ohio

I moved from Ohio to take a position as an endowed chair at Middle Tennessee State University in Murfreesboro. Whenever I would say something, my secretary would remind me, "Now Dr. Kick, in the South we do it this way or we say it that way." One day in the Sunday paper there was a big ad that said *WIDOWS ONLY*. I thought it was going to be for a research project, and I was interested because I was a widow. Instead, it was a personal ad for a man seeking a woman. I cut it out, brought it to work, and told my secretary, "Now look at this. We don't do this in the North. We would never do this in Ohio." To which she replied, "Who cares what you do in Ohio? It says physically fit and financially sound—you should answer it!"

I was uneasy about meeting someone because anything could happen. I didn't know him. I didn't know anyone who knew him. I thought he could be a murderer or a rapist, but every day my secretary brought it up and asked if I answered the ad. When she realized I wasn't going to answer it, she decided to do it herself. Taking an old picture of me from the bulletin board in my office with a baby in each arm, she sent it to "The Jazzy Senior" along with the comment, "I can walk and chew gum at the same time so I'm the one you're looking for." Surprisingly, he answered and invited me to lunch. My daughter told me not to do it. My secretary told me to do it. He was seventy-one at the time—we have the same birthday, but we are eleven years apart. I thought anyone who has to advertise for a woman can't be much. But it turned out that he spent his life in Arabia and Algeria as a geophysicist, he was a widower, and the newspaper wrote the ad for him. This was 1990.

On the phone he sounded pretty nice—like he had a couple of brain cells. He could carry on a conversation. He looked pretty good in his picture. And he wanted to take me to Sunday brunch. I figured I couldn't go wrong. If I didn't like him I could tell him to be on his way. I suggested that we meet at a Holiday Inn where there was a nice brunch. I told him what I would be wearing and what kind of car I had. When he saw me pull up he came out to the car and said we couldn't eat there because they were remodeling. I thought, *Oh here we go*. At that point I suggested we go in to the hotel so that someone would see me with him. Turned out he was telling the truth. They really were remodeling. I gave his phone number and picture to my daughter and said, "If you don't hear from me in an hour call the police." She said, "No. You got yourself into this." So I gave it to my secretary. I almost forgot to call her to tell her everything was okay.

After that he invited me to go places—always on a Sunday. I thought he might be married. My secretary told me that I could find out by inviting him to Thanksgiving dinner. So I did and he agreed. My son-in-law talked to him while I was in the kitchen and eventually came to me and said, "You want to know why he only comes on Sunday? He drives four hours each way to see you."

We met in October, he proposed in May, and we got married in July. We were married for nineteen years, and it was a good nineteen years without regrets. This experience taught me that when you think you're getting a pig in a poke, there could be a silver lining. I thought I was going to brunch and have a cup of coffee and some eggs, and that would be that. It doesn't always turn out that good, but I was very fortunate. You still have to be cautious. Joe turned out to be a good Southern gentleman.

Despite my own losses and heartbreaks, I helped others through theirs and built a community of caring and loving allies of younger generations. Now, at age ninety-four, I have a contingent of young friends who love and care for me in many, many more ways than I could possibly imagine or even expect. Acts of kindness are not forgotten—they come back to you with interest.

Mollie Pier

1920
Los Angeles, California
Died: April 28, 2016

Don't rush into marriage. Live together
for a few years and see if it works.

Michele S. | April 5, 1937
Brittany, France

Dont judge people. You don't know what's
going on in their lives or why they think
or act the way that they do.

Guadalupe Ocampo Zepeda | June 11, 1921
Toluca, Estado de México

Hope Heumann | February 19, 1928 / O'Fallon, Illinois

The experience Hope shared with having a transsexual son teaches us all the meaning of love and acceptance.

I had just one child, a daughter. When she was little, my husband's sister bought her a really darling little doll with a pink dress. She would throw that doll from one end of the room to the other. I didn't put any significance to it, but I do remember it. Then in high school I wanted to buy her some luggage with little flowers on it, and we had the biggest fight over it. Little things went on that you see, but you don't see.

In the 1970s when my daughter was eighteen, she said she wanted a sex change. I was bewildered. My husband always blamed me for the fact that she was gay or this or that. I didn't know what to do. All I could do was pray. My husband and I just couldn't see going along with it at that age in case she didn't like it and changed her mind. So she lived the "gay life."

There was no one to talk to about it. You don't want to see anyone because you can't talk about it. You can't fuss with her. That's just who she was. She and I were good buddies. My husband wasn't that good to her. I kept saying we had to keep the contact open.

He was someone who couldn't trust anyone or be close to anyone. Now, I have a son. He completed gender reassignment in 2015.

To keep going, you need to be grateful for everything you have and count your blessings. Try to accept the way things are and make the best of them. Don't get into feeling sorry for yourself. No one wants to hear you complain. Accept your limitations even though it's not easy. Friends and certain people you really trust will be there for you. Accept people as best you can. As you get older you realize you really aren't as relevant as you once were. I've come to realize we are only here temporarily, and all you can do is the best you can. We all make mistakes.

I would advise young women to develop your inner self even though there is so much going on. Be true to yourself. Listen to your inner self. Develop your spirituality. Don't accept less than what you really want.

142

Life is a wonderful adventure and each of us is part of its story. Always feel blessed for children, family, and many friends who have contributed to our joyous lifetime journey. Relish good old memories that visit us late at night. Finally, be optimistic for the future no matter how old you may be. Each day look forward to what life might bring our way.

Jean Hensleigh | 1934
Ann Arbor, Michigan

Don't complain about what you have to do. Just get it done. Children see this and learn from it.

Charlotte Ziporyn | September 12, 1931
Chicago, Illinois

It's better to have tried and failed than to never have tried at all.

Ellie Prischak | October 16, 1927
Youngstown, Ohio

Don't lose your femininity. Don't give up your basic personality to be more like a man.

Peggy Cutting | August 26, 1931
Tulsa, Oklahoma

During our eighth grade lessons Sister Teresa Maura would constantly connect common courtesy with social justice. She would say:

Be good to those coming along behind. Hold the door. Wait for the slowpoke. Help with her bag. Don't let your classmate fail if you can help her. Give little kids a break.
The world will be better!

Sister Teresa Maura | 1910
Brooklyn, New York
Died: 1975

Never turn down God's work.
We are blessed and will be blessed.
What we have now, we got from Him.
Even though He never asks for a return,
we should feel grateful if we can do it,
especially when we have the talent.

Betsy W. Tirie-Ratu | June 19, 1931
Menado, Indonesia

The best piece of parenting advice
I ever got was from my mother:
Never wish your child's life away.
She was right. We need to enjoy
each day and stage with whatever
it brings. My son's youth passed in
the blink of an eye. But thanks to
my mom, I enjoyed every day
at every stage, knowing that today
would soon be a sweet memory.

Shirley Parker | March 19, 1932
Rail Road Flat, California

Hard work and perseverance
will get you where you
want to go.

Delores Vines | 1932
Leesville, Louisiana

Don't take things too seriously.
You make a mountain out
of a molehill.

Lilian Dorothy Whelan | October 10, 1929
Harlem, New York

To know who you really are
is by being grateful.

Siti Sofiah Thahir | February 2, 1924
Subang, Indonesia
Died: August 19, 2005

As an eighty-two year old, I appreciate what I have learned in my physical journey this lifetime. I have come to understand that love is the constant! The ONE is all there is and we are all part it. I believe that age is a state of mind. I do not intend to accept the belief that physical and mental decline is inevitable with aging. I maintain my physical well-being and mental acuity by doing yoga, swimming every night, and continuing to work online daily.

I have been a spiritual explorer and have learned the power of my thinking. I know that my thoughts create my reality. My personal checks have the words *The Thoughts of This Moment Create My Future* printed on them. Thoughts do indeed become things. They lead to feelings, which lead to actions, which lead to results. The Universe always says yes! I have also learned that believing is seeing, and that seeing is not believing. What I believe determines what I will perceive. All is choice, and how I think determines my life.

I understand that a review of my belief systems with the release of those that no longer serve me are important to do regularly, for as within, so without. I recognize the value of doing intentions and meditating on them, and I do this practice regularly. I am channeling from astral and causal levels with automatic writing each evening. My book *A Nightly Word*, with pragmatic spiritual principles, was recently published. My intention is to share and teach the spiritual knowledge I have learned, including the channeled information, with those who are open and receptive to it.

And finally my intention is to experience a happy, healthy, fulfilling retirement with all the dollars I need to meet all expenses; to travel; to enjoy theater, art, and music with a complementary and compatible male companion; to continue my spiritual exploration and teach spiritual truths; and to be there to help my children and grandchildren. And so it is.

Pat Gomavitz | December 3, 1932
Milwaukee, Wisconsin

Susana "Sucy" Stevenson | December 24, 1933
Tegucigalpa, Honduras

My parents had me take ballet lessons and poise lessons. We had to educate others about what Hispanics were capable of. They encouraged my education and wanted me to achieve my goals. There was the expectation that I would be educated. My father had the concept of independence, and to get it you had to be educated.

I was engaged at twenty-one and married at twenty-three. I wanted to be a doctor, but my husband wanted to be a dentist. I was a UCLA graduate and had been accepted to medical school. So, I gave up school. My father didn't speak to me for seven years after I quit. I thought it was better to be the wife of a doctor than to be a doctor. We got no support from my family. I was a Latin girl from a protective family. No one thought the marriage would last. We've been married now for fifty-eight years. It's been a happy life and I have no regrets.

When David got his dental degree, we went to Alaska to work with the Alaskan Natives. I taught them Spanish so that they could get better jobs in Seattle. They needed a second language. I also taught them office skills like typing. I worked in my husband's dental office and went to school at night to learn how to be a dental hygienist. I ran the dental office in Sitka, Alaska. I'm still working now because I don't know how to do anything else. Now I worry how I will adjust when my darling dies. I don't know how to be a widow. We share everything. We buy a sandwich for lunch and cut it in half.

My advice for young women is to make up your mind what you want to do and have patience and perseverance —and you will succeed. Be focused.

Be grateful for each day and take
advantage of every opportunity that
comes your way. You may be surprised
at where these opportunities lead you.
Be aware of the mysteries and beauty
of nature—trees, flowers, animals—
and take nothing for granted.

Sister Joan Kehn, O.P. | February 21, 1937
Toledo, Ohio

Yvonne Richmond

March 20, 1934
Selma, Alabama

A friend of mine used to say, it's never too late to rewrite your script. Yvonne Richmond shows us how to do just that with courage and confidence.

Dad was a farmer who grew cotton, corn, potatoes, and ribbon cane. He started as a sharecropper but eventually bought his own land. He was great at coordinating and organizing things. Mom was seventeen and Dad was nineteen when they married. I was the ninth of ten children. All the children weren't around at the same time, but you could get lost in a family that size.

It seems like Mama was in the kitchen all the time. We were a planned community of kids. We all knew what we had to do before we could go off and play. Washing dishes was one of my chores. We had no running water and used a kerosene lamp for light. Papa bought a wood-burning Roper Stove and you would put a tub on the side to put water in. Then the stove would heat it up and you could use the water to wash the dishes. I have a dishwashing hangover now from washing so many dishes.

When I was a little girl and I planted my first seeds, I was so proud when they popped up. I thought, *Look what I made!* We couldn't possibly use all of the fruits and vegetables that we grew, but Papa didn't like us to "peddle." That's when you go into town and sell what you grew to people on the street. So Mama would put everything in baskets and go into stores like Boston Bargain and Teppler's and sell to the shop owners. That wasn't considered peddling. At the end of the year whatever was left over Papa would leave in the field for the workers and others to come and take. That was called "scrapping." Some of the scrappers would use it

for their own families and others would peddle it in town. Papa gave to the community this way.

One time my mother told my father that a neighbor's daughter was pregnant. She didn't have any boyfriends or any brothers. So Papa went and talked to the girl's father. I think he was a social worker before I knew what a social worker was.

The most vivid memory I have from childhood was in 1948 when I was about fourteen years old. I was home with my younger brother, my sister who was eight months pregnant, and my four-year-old nephew, who was in bed with me. A tornado hit the house and took the roof right off. When I looked up into the night I saw a twisting ball with flames coming out of it. It destroyed the entire house. The only thing left standing was the chimney. And when the tornado left, the sky cleared and you could see the moon so bright.

Considering there were no phones, word spread quickly and people started coming from all over the county. Even if we did have phones, prejudice was so bad that emergency help might not have come. I was burned so badly that I was in and out of consciousness. I woke up in the hospital with two doctors arguing over me. One, a black doctor, said my arm was so badly damaged that they should just take it off. Another, a woman doctor, said she didn't want to leave this young girl with only one arm. I spoke up and said, "Don't take it off," then passed out again. So when I woke up the first thing I did was check to make sure I still had my arm. I still have the scars, but I have my arm!

In 1948, the Ku Klux Klan was raging. I never saw hangings and burnings, but I knew they happened. One young man returned from the military as a Captain. He went into a store to buy something, and instead of saying "yes sir" to the clerk, he said, "yeah." They beat him to death.

We were taught that there were certain places we just shouldn't go. If we saw something wrong—or something that even might be wrong—to run the other way. Because my father was friends with some of the white men, they would warn him in advance of the places to avoid. Those white people didn't take part in it, but they didn't stop it either. About my father, they used to say, "Mannie Smith is a smart nigger. He's got as much as a white man." But it didn't matter if you were in Selma or Cleveland or Chicago or Los Angeles. Prejudice was everywhere.

After I graduated from high school I wanted to go to Selma University. But Papa said we didn't have the money. So I moved to Cleveland to live with my brother to see if I could save enough money to go to college. When I left, Papa told me not to have babies before I was married and to go back to school as soon as I could. My first job was at Barnes Department Store at 71st and Central, and from there I went to work in the dietary department of St. Luke's Hospital. By now it was about 1953, and I got married and started having my own children. I stayed home to raise them for a while but we needed more money. My husband was a barber. So I got a job at a pharmacy.

I did fine at the pharmacy. I worked there for about eleven years off and on. But I was separated now and my three boys were growing up. I was opening the store, closing the store, working as head clerk, and doing everything. I even saved the store in the late 1960s when the rioters came in and asked us to buy an African flag and my boss refused. I grabbed money from the cash register, gave it to the rioters, then took that flag upstairs and hung it out the window. Only the stores that had the flag hanging weren't burned down. So when I went and asked for a raise that I thought I had earned, I was surprised to hear, "You're already at the top of your pay grade." I don't know how I did it but I turned, got my time card and clocked out. I just walked out!

I called a friend to pick me up and I told him the story. This was in August. He drove me to the college and told me to go in and ask for a grant. I was lucky that the woman could see I was older than most of the students, and she wanted to help me. I said I wanted to study mental health. She said I definitely qualified, and within two days I had my schedule.

I was nervous going back to school because it had been twenty-five years since I graduated from high school. Then once I got to class, I realized these kids couldn't read and write! One of the professors could see I was a good student and gave me a job working as a peer counselor in the mental health office. On weekends, I worked at a little café to make ends meet. Eventually I got three associate's degrees before going on to Ursuline College and getting a bachelor's in behavioral science.

I always knew I wanted to go back to college. I kept asking myself, *What are you waiting for?* When I quit my job, deep down inside I said, *Don't use anger unless you can make it work for you.* That's what I did when I quit my job. I made my anger work for me.

If you realistically have the wherewithal to do what you want—then do it! Recognize what's realistic. Do the financial analysis. Look at who you have behind you to help. Have dreams, but be realistic.

My advice to young women is to ask yourself, *What do I want to do?* To succeed you have to do what you like and be realistic about it. Be kind and generous without it hurting you. Be careful how much you give away—save some of it for yourself. When things are going badly, be conscious of it, but not anxious over it.

Never think you know it all.

Never run for a bus. There will always be another one.

Adelina Malina Sjogen Nelson | July 30, 1883
Gottenberg, Sweden
Died: 1983

Sue Doody | September 22, 1934
Dayton, Ohio

*Calling at the appointed time to speak with
the eighty-one-year old owner of Lindey's
Restaurant in Columbus, Ohio, a woman
answered the phone who I assumed, based
on the strength and vitality in her voice, was
most likely an assistant or her daughter. Nope.
I was speaking with Sue herself. She is a living
testament to the fact that if you do what you
love and stay active throughout your life, you'll
enter your later years with the grace, warmth,
and the mental sharpness of Sue Doody.*

My husband was a successful businessman and a
professor at Ohio State. I taught school to put him
through his doctorate. In fact, I typed his dissertation.
In 1976, when we'd been married about twenty years,
he told me he wanted a divorce. I didn't think I'd ever be
divorced. It was kind of a shock that he walked out.
He went on to marry four other women, so I don't feel
so bad. I never married again. I just jumped into being
mother to our four children and a business owner.

I wanted to do something but I didn't know what I
wanted to do. I didn't want to go back to teaching.
I did always have an interest in food from the time I was
growing up. We traveled a lot and would always eat
in the best restaurants. Then Julia Child became a
great person to learn from, and I would cook right
along with her. Other kids' Moms would make a
sandwich out of chicken. At Sue's house, they had
crepes with leftover chicken!

So, I started doing catering and taught classes in
French cooking in my house. I cooked through Julia
Child's book and television program. It helped me
emotionally. I wanted to be home with the children,
and this was a good way to do it.

In the late seventies, Columbus had terrible food. They
served canned green beans at the best restaurants.
People didn't know specialty cooking or cooking with
fresh veggies and wine. People kept telling me that I
was a good cook, so I opened my own restaurant in
1980. I wouldn't have been as successful without sup-
portive children and family. My ex-husband helped
financially and in other ways. Still, it was tough.

When I bought the restaurant, it was called the Lin-
denhoff. I named the restaurant Lindey's because it
had a large linden tree behind it. It was in German
Village near Columbus. The Germans brought linden

seeds with them and the trees did well in our climate.

I tell people, whatever business you're interested in, go into it and try to get a job with it first, or at least go to observe or follow them around. I didn't do this before starting my business, but it helps. Had I done that, I would have known how much hard work it was and the time it takes. I don't know if it would have discouraged me. I might not have gone out on a limb. I knew what I wanted and how I wanted it, and I didn't know any place in Columbus that had what I wanted. Like an Upper East Side café in New York—quality food made from scratch, white tablecloths, hardwood floors. I also wanted to sell local art. Well, it got to the point where I was doing that instead of food. I didn't want to be an art dealer, I wanted to be a restauranteur.

I didn't know if the restaurant was going to make it. "How does this den mother think she's going to make a success of this white elephant?" the bank laughed when I asked for money. I had to have my former husband co-sign. Now I have a good reputation. I spent fourteen- to fifteen-hour days at my restaurant. I'd race home and feed the kids and go back and stay until closing time. It was tough as a single Mom with some children still at home. I tried to support them in what they were doing. I look back and wonder, *How in the world did I do this?* I didn't get involved in the nonprofits and the boards until after the restaurant was successful and I wanted to give back to the community that had supported my restaurant.

I rely on my faith a lot and meditate. I read a lot. I'm really strong. **I have a great faith in God and I think there's something more on this earth that we aren't let into. Things will be revealed at a later time. Ultimately, things are good, but when bad things happen that we don't have an understanding of, we will find out the reason at a later time.**

People love to talk about themselves. If you learn to be curious about people, you'll always be liked.

September 26, 1920
Torrance, California
Died: July 12, 1993

Don't ever say, "I can't." Don't ever say, "I am old." Keep on going to the gym and stay actively involved in at least one thing about which you are passionate. If you are lucky, that will also include your husband.

Nancy Mannes | June 12, 1930
Bethesda, Maryland

You can use almost any measure when you speak of success—you can measure it in fancy homes or big cars or dresses, but the measure of your real success is one you cannot spend: it's the way your kids describe you when they're talking to a friend.

Florence Bennett | July 9, 1927
Cleveland, Ohio

Aspire to be your best self. No one else can
do that, no one else can be that, and no one
else can tell you what that is.

Bobbye Erhardt

December 27, 1928
Corpus Christi, Texas
Died: March 18, 2009

When you awaken each morning, choose to
be happy and make it a good day, be a loyal
friend and you will have lots of them,
and never jeopardize your integrity.

Tibby Heno | November 22, 1942
New Orleans, Louisiana

164

Don't wait to do the things you want to do. Make plans and work toward them. There will always be things that seem more pressing or practical in the moment, but don't let them get in your way.
Do it now!

Dr. Ann Roulet | March 7, 1933
St. Joseph, Missouri

Yo Zeimen | August 7, 1940
Los Angeles, California

In 2005 when I was diagnosed with breast cancer, I was introduced to the Appearance Center at Huntington Hospital in Pasadena, California. There I met a tiny Japanese woman who would not only shave my head and tailor a wig for me when the time came but who would also become a dear friend. As I got to know her in the intervening years, I learned she had an amazing story to tell about resilience, faith, and how you can choose to live happily ever after.

My parents were in a traditional Japanese arranged marriage. Their families knew one another from the time they were born in Honolulu and when they later moved to Japan. All of their lives, it was a given that they would get married. First they had my brother, who is ten years older than me, and then my sister who is seven years older. I was born soon after World War II broke out. By now, my family was living in Los Angeles.

After the Japanese bombed Pearl Harbor in 1942, my family was relocated to a Japanese Internment Camp. First we were sent to Santa Anita racetrack to be processed, and then we were shipped to Gila River Camp in Arizona.* I was less than two years old when we went, so I don't remember too much about it. Sometimes I wonder if I actually remember certain things or if I was told them. One thing I do think I

remember is the big gong that was hit when it was time for meals. Everyone would start running toward the mess hall. I can remember being carried on someone's shoulder and looking back and seeing all these people running. My mother told me that before going to the camp, we had three days to get rid of everything we owned. We could only take what we could carry. My brother now jokes that he told my mother to leave me and take something more important, but she didn't listen. I seem to recall playing with my brother and sister and a man who would squat with a stick in the old Japanese way and tell stories. I also remember it snowing and a woman telling me that a man was taking pictures. He wasn't supposed to and would be punished if he was caught. Some of the men who were Americans wanted to go to war and fight. A few of them were released to go and be translators.

I remember we all lived a tin house that was shaped like a hut. It would make noise when it rained, and there were spaces I could look out of. It was just one big area, and there were some kind of curtains for dividers. I had no sense that anything was wrong because it's all that I knew. After the war, my Dad was very bitter. He wanted to be a chiropractor but that dream was shattered. When the war was over, they gave us ten dollars and a train ticket to Union Station in Los Angeles. We got a hotel room in Skid Row. We used to call it the Cockroach Hotel. There were all Japanese families staying there, and there was one community kitchen. This was when I started going to school. My mother went to work for a paper manufacturer and my father became a produce man. In those days, if you were Japanese you were either a gardener or in produce.

My parents never really shared their feelings with me. It wasn't so much because of the internment; it's just how the old Japanese were. You knew they loved you but not because they said it or showed it. There really was no affection. I remember going up to my mother to hug her and she would just brush me away. Or I'd tried to hold my Dad's hand and he would shoo me off. I think my sister was most affected by it all. She blamed everything wrong in her life on being the middle child and getting the brunt of things. She hated my Dad, but I don't know what happened. Something big happened but no one talked about it. It's been twenty-five years since she stopped talking to me and my brother. I've tried calling her many times, but she won't talk to me.

Starting school was horrifying. I didn't know how to speak English, and I was teased a lot. I didn't know what they were saying but I knew it wasn't nice—we were taunted.

After a while, my Aunt, who had a boarding house in Pasadena, passed away. My parents took it over and we moved there. I still remember it was located at 40 Valley Street. Now it's a doctor's office. My mother worked hard taking in the boarders. They were all Japanese gardeners! My father stayed working in produce. She got up at 4:00 a.m. and made their breakfast and lunch. Every Saturday I had to help her clean the rooms, and at night I would wash dishes.

As a teenager I was a rebel. I'd go out with friends to parties and get cheap wine and get sick. We'd drink over at the park by the boarding house. There weren't a lot of police around back then to stop you. I had cousins in Pasadena, but for some reason they didn't like me so I gravitated to the Blacks, Hispanics, and Whites. The people I hung out with were on the tough side. The Mexicans had their little groups. They weren't really gangs—they were just trying to act tough.

High school was a really unhappy time. I barely skimmed through. I didn't know what I wanted to do or in which direction I wanted to go. I didn't graduate—

I dropped out in my senior year. School was hard for me with English not being my first language. My mother made my sister tutor me, and when no one was looking she'd hit me over the head with a book and call me stupid. Mom and Dad were so busy working they didn't pay much attention to me. So I believed I really was stupid and became introverted. It's why I don't like to speak in front of groups.

My Dad was verbally abusive to my mother. I know he cheated on her. In the boarding house we only had a pay phone, and his girlfriends would call him. I used to tell them to stop calling.

My sister became a hairdresser. I wanted to be a nurse but my Mom told me to do what my sister was doing, so I became a hairdresser too. When I was seventeen, I went to Al Tate's Beauty Academy on the Corner of Colorado and Fair Oaks Boulevard within walking distance from my home. Now it's a Crate and Barrel. Back then there were all winos around there and we'd have to step over them, but they were harmless. While going to beauty school, I worked at Huntington Memorial Hospital in the cafeteria. That's where I had my two girls too.

I met my husband at a party. This guy walked in and I said he was cute. My friend Connie said, "He's not cute, he's my brother." We were together for seven or eight months and then I got pregnant. We got married because we would have done so anyway. My parents wouldn't come to the wedding and disowned me because I was marrying a white man—they didn't know I was pregnant. It was just a small wedding. My husband's parents were there, but no one from my side of the family came. We were married at the First Presbyterian Church on Lake Avenue in Pasadena. When I told my mother I was going to have a baby, she welcomed me back.

I don't feel as if I ever really had support from other people. I just went on my own journey. My husband was a forklift driver and I was home caring for our daughter. We were saving for a house and were happy together. Then, about three years after we were married, he got together with some friends from high school and started doing heroin. He said it was just a weekend thing. I didn't know how to help him. I finally figured out he was hooked when he lost his job and started selling drugs. He wanted to quit so badly. He told me to take all of my clothes and the car and stay with my mother for three days. I did, and when I got back he was gone.

He really battled drugs. I left him, but I came back because I loved him and I was young and foolish. That's when I got pregnant again with our second daughter. I was working as a hairdresser by now and he stayed home taking care of the kids. I'll never forget the day I got a call from the police. My husband was busted for selling drugs. They said I could come home and get the kids or they would be sent to social services. He was sentenced to serve three years in jail. While we were waiting for him to report to jail, I got pregnant again. I was about twenty-three years old and already supporting the family. I didn't tell my husband. I didn't want to give up this baby, but I didn't know how I could take care of three kids. I mentioned it to a nun at church and she took over. She convinced me that giving up the baby was the best thing to do. When the baby was born, I looked at him and said, "I can't give him up." The nuns said that he was going to a good family. The father was a dentist who could give him everything I couldn't. Looking back now, I know I made the right choice. It was the only thing I could do. The County had to tell my husband and get his signature on the adoption papers.

Raising kids alone was tough. It's a cold, cruel world, and I had no one to help. I was always private and proud. I had some friends, but because I was always so busy taking care of my family I didn't call them, and eventually they left. I was working two jobs. During the day I worked in a salon and at night I worked as a cocktail waitress. Either my mother or a babysitter watched the kids. Then one day, I couldn't walk. I went to the doctor and he said I was exhausted. I was going on three hours of sleep a night.

Once I started visiting my husband in jail, the feelings I had for him changed. Something came over me. I didn't like him anymore. I divorced him. When he got out, he wanted to get back together but I had a boyfriend. Over the years, he kept popping up like a thorn in my side. I let him see the kids when he was clean and sober. I was connected to his mother because she was the kids' grandmother. He died alone in an empty house of a seizure. The only regret I have is not knowing how to help him.

For the next forty years I worked and raised my daughters. I married again, but I knew what I really wanted was a father for my girls. I divorced him, too. A few years ago, my grandson died at twenty-four of a heroin overdose. He was a good boy. He played football in high school and broke his shoulder. The doctors gave him pain medications, and that's when it started. My daughter told them there was a history of substance abuse in the family. Both his father and his grandfather were substance abusers. He had the genetic background.

In 2007, the phone rang and a woman asked if I was Yo Zeimen and if I had a son. I thought, *Someone was playing a joke on me*. She asked if the child was born at St. Luke's Hospital. I said, "Oh, my God." My son had been searching for me, and this company finally found me. I asked when I could see him and we made a plan for the following Sunday when he would be back in town from a business trip.

I called my girls and told them. They always knew they had a brother. There were times when they wanted to find him, but I didn't feel I had the right after giving him up. I was scared and happy at the same time. My sister-in-law asked how I could be sure it was him. I wanted to believe it was him. When Sunday came, we were all crowded into one space looking out this little window. When he parked and got out of the car, I couldn't look anymore. When he walked in the door, I looked at him and said, "Son!" and held him for the longest time. I was on top of the world. I was in the most beautiful place. My dream came true. I had always wondered where he was and if he was okay.

We sat around the kitchen table and talked. My girls had a few little doubts and he had questions for us. He wondered too if this was really his family. Then I got out a picture that I had of him as an infant. It had been given to me at the hospital. It turned out that his adoptive mother had that same picture, so he had seen it. That cinched it. It was an over-the-top feeling. Like a miracle. Thirty-nine years had passed and now he was raising his own son. He's such a good daddy.

As for what's next? My oldest grandson lives with me now. He became depressed when his brother died. He's still working that out. My goal is to help him get back on his feet. After that I want to make the Appearance Center bigger. I'm old now, and I have to find some people whom I can teach what I do. There are other Appearance Centers, but they are not as professionally run as this one. A lot of cosmetologists ask me if they could do this. But it's not just a job. I'm so protective of this. I don't want someone who will just treat it like a job.

I had volunteered for about seven years at the City of Hope. I knew I wanted to help cancer patients. Then Huntington Hospital approached me about starting an Appearance Center. I said no, because I lived too far away from Huntington. A year later they called and actually had money to do this, so I came to set it up. I started a place where I could give clients hope. When someone says you're going to lose your hair, it's like hitting a woman over the head with a hammer. I show them that the doctors are helping them on the inside and that they can look beautiful on the outside. I sell head covers, wigs, and give them makeup do's and dont's .

The Appearance Center makes me realize that I'm not the only one who has suffered. Through my religion I am at peace with myself. I'm still here. Thank God for that!

Author's Note: Following the bombing of Pearl Harbor in 1942, during one of the most shameful periods in United States history, the American government forced the incarceration of over 110,000 people of Japanese ancestry into what were euphemistically referred to as "Relocation Camps." Most of these people lived along the Pacific Coast of the country and the majority were U.S. citizens who had built businesses, owned homes, had pets, and were productive members of society. During their incarceration from 1942 to 1946, all of their possessions were confiscated, leaving them nothing to go home to. It wasn't until 1988 that the government apologized for the internment and authorized a payment of $20,000 to each individual camp survivor. It was admitted that the incarceration was based on "race prejudice, war hysteria, and a failure of political leadership."

ACKNOWLEDGMENTS

First and foremost, I thank all of the women who took the time to speak with me about their life experiences. I am so grateful for your candor and trust.

I also thank all of the people who submitted stories, wisdom, and quotes from the ageless women in their lives, both living and having passed away. I appreciate the time you took to dig out your pictures and provide me with wisdom from your loved ones. I'm sorry if image quality, size, or space wouldn't allow us to use the picture you sent in print, but most are posted on the website.

Traveling around the country looking for women to interview, I had help and referrals from quite a few people. Thank you, Rob Lucarelli, at the Judson Smart Living Community in Cleveland, Ohio, for arranging interviews with your residents. Itje Suryono, Jane Moore, Susan Hunter Hancock, Donna Croft, Tibby Heno, Mary Ellen Hill, Linda Carpenter, and Joanne Wanstreet, thank you for your invaluable connections and contributions. I apologize in advance to anyone I've overlooked. Everyone's assistance was a gift.

Sister Beverly Bobola, thank you for the day spent with me at the Mother House of the Adrian Dominicans. Speaking with the sisters and learning more about your order was enlightening and refreshing.

Kim Lim and Skyhorse Publishing, thank you for sharing Ageless Women, Timeless Wisdom with a broad spectrum of readers.

Thank you to Karen Flannery for being my first reader, a sounding board, and great friend.

Pam, thank you for never thinking my myriad ideas are foolish and for encouraging me to chase after all of them.

And last but not least, I thank Lisa Graves for so beautifully bringing to life the words I transcribed with illustrations that complement the content. I truly could not have done this without you and am grateful beyond words.

SYNTHIA SAINT JAMES

The author gratefully acknowledges the generous contribution of Synthia Saint James, creator of "Grandmother Spirit," the painting that graces the back cover of this book.

The painting is the embodiment of ageless women everywhere who lovingly impart their collective wisdom. Synthia is a world-renowned multicultural visual artist, award-winning author, and keynote speaker. She is most celebrated for designing the first Kwanzaa Stamp for the United States Postal Service in 1997, for which she received a History Maker Award, and the international cover art for Terry McMillan's book *Waiting to Exhale*. Synthia has garnered numerous awards over her forty-five-year career, including the prestigious Trumpet Award, an Honorary Doctorate Degree from Saint Augustine's College, and Women Who Dared Award, to name just a few.

To learn more about Synthia Saint James, purchase a giclée of "Grandmother Spirit," and enjoy her creative world, visit her website: ***synthiasaintjames.com***

Dr. Lois Frankel

Lois is the author of numerous bestselling books, including the business bible for women, *Nice Girls Don't Get the Corner Office*. After a career making a living as a consultant, executive coach, keynote speaker, and author, she now applies the wit and wisdom she garnered during own well-lived life to projects that make a difference in the lives of women and girls. Although she continues to write and speak to women's groups around the world, Lois spends more time helping to grow Bloom Again Foundation, the nonprofit she started with colleagues and friends, to coach young women via telephone and email on how to achieve their career goals, and building the Crafty Sisters Collection, a place for women artists to sell their handmade work. A native New Yorker, she currently enjoys living in Southern California where she can garden year round and take her rescue dog, Maddie, on long walks just about 365 days a year.

To contact or learn more about Lois visit one of her websites:
drloisfrankel.com
craftysisterscollection.com
bloomagain.org

To submit your wisdom or that of a woman seventy years old or better go to *www.wordsofwisdomproject.com.*

Lisa Graves

Lisa Graves is the author and illustrator of the *Women in History* series. She is also the creator of Historywitch.com, a site dedicated to illustrations of history's greatest and most fascinating characters. Lisa has published several grown-up coloring books, as well as the illustrated medieval cookbook *A Thyme and Place*, co-authored with Tricia Cohen. She lives in Medway, Massachusetts.

historywitch.com
lisagravesdesign.com